Crackerjack Selling Secrets

–

Persuasion Strategies of the Most Successful Sales, Marketing, and Negotiation Pros Who Ever Lived

ISBN: 9781549579790

By Ben Settle
Published by MakeRight Publishing, Inc.
©2017 Ben Settle

Disclaimer and Copyright Information

Before reading, please take a second and go to:

BenSettle.com

... to access the hundreds of FREE tips and hours of audio content waiting there for you. Plus, if you join the mailing list you will also get a free (digital pdf) issue of the prestigious ($97/month) "Email Players" newsletter.

Table of Contents

Introduction

As loathe as I am to admit it, one of my favorite movies is *Star Wars: Revenge of the Sith.*

One scene I like is the Anakin Skywalker and Obi Wan Kenobi duel. This when they are on a small floating "platform" of debris over a river of molten metal fiercely trying to kill each other with their light sabers. Seeing a way to escape, Obi Wan Kenobi suddenly jumps to the "river" bank, leaving Anakin on the floating platform.

Obi Wan warns him, "It's over Anakin. I've got the high ground."

Anakin—arrogant, power drunk and thinking he's invulnerable due to his sudden power surge from the dark side of the force—jumps anyway. And even though Obi Wan is a less skilled fighter and swordsman, because he had the high ground, he was able to easily (with one movement) cut off both of Anakin's legs and his arm—rendering him broken and defeated.

Well, guess what?

This is a perfect example of what happens in sales, too—

When You Have
the "High Ground"

When you take the high ground in business—you don't need to be the "best" sales man.

You don't need to have the most resources and financial backing.

And, you can win even when competing against more skilled sales, marketing, and copywriting pros. I call this kind of selling—where you take the high ground focusing on proven principles based on sound psychological laws (instead of just tricks and tactics)—

"Crackerjack Selling"

The text book definition of "crackerjack" means to be exceptionally good at something.

And that is what this book is all about: Being exceptionally good at selling—regardless of your skills (or lack of skills) now. You can do it by not focusing on the latest manipulative tips and tricks... but instead using principles that are in perfect harmony with what people want and how they make buying decisions. The principles in this book have been used for centuries by the world's most persuasive sales, marketing, and negotiating pros. And they can be applied to any kind of selling — whether you're face-to-face selling, tele-marketing, direct response copywriting, direct marketing, negotiating, setting up joint ventures, using social media, email marketing... and everything in between. If you sell, market, or advertise in any way, shape or form—then this book will (if you apply it) give you an enormous advantage over everyone you compete against.

You won't have to rely on selling "choke holds" and fancy-shmancy closes.

You won't have to worry about rejection.

And, in almost every case, you will...

**Close Far MORE Sales
With A Lot LESS Effort
Every Time**

How can I be so sure?

Because these are selling "principles"—and not necessarily "tactics." (Although there are a few tactic-based secrets in here, too). They are not based on persistence, having a thick skin or knowing 100 ways to magically close a sale. Instead, these are 101 of the simplest and most reliable selling principles ever invented. They are based on common sense and the laws of human behavior. And not on manipulation, "black hat" tactics or any of that nonsense.

Frankly, these secrets worked 1,000 years ago.

They work today.

And, they will work 1,000 years from now.

Plus, here's the best part:

Although there are 101 secrets in this book, you do not need to know them all. You can have massive success simply picking the ones you like most—that are aligned with your personality and selling style—and using them almost exclusively. And if you sell for a living (and if you are in business you do SELL for a living, whether you like it or not) this book will make the process far easier and more profitable for you.

These secrets have certainly changed my life.

And if you apply them, I have no doubt they will do the same for you.

-Ben Settle
Bandon, OR

P.S. Although I strongly recommend reading the first 7 chapters no matter what—you do not have to read this book in any specific order. It is designed so you can open it to any page, at any time, and find a powerful sales tip you can apply to your business at will. Just go through the table of contents or flip through the pages and read whatever stands out. Some tips are interconnected and if one tip is related to another (or strengthens another) it is noted. Each "chapter" is no more than a page or two long.

And they are designed for you to read, absorb, and learn them extremely fast.

So, feel free to jump through it, skipping, reading, and focusing on whatever suits you. You are in no way bound to read this book cover to cover or in any specific order to extract "gold" from it.

Crackerjack Selling Secret #1:
The World's Most "Un-Sexiest" Sales Secret

This first Crackerjack Selling Secret is the most *important* in this book.

It is the "engine" that makes the other secrets work. Without an engine, you can roll a car down a hill and push it, but it will be slow and hard. With an engine, you can drive and get wherever you want with ease and almost zero effort.

And it's the same with this first Crackerjack Selling secret.

The rest of the secrets from here on out will always work.

But not nearly as well or *consistently*.

And, although it may sound hokey, if you use it in your selling endeavors, I think you will be pleasantly surprised by what happens.

Anyway, here it is:

Sincerely *Caring* About
Those You Sell To.

Why is this so all-fired important?

Two reasons:

First, really *caring* about someone before trying to sell them anything ensures you are always doing things for the right reasons. If you care about someone, you will want what is best for them. And let's face it: There are some cases where what you sell may NOT be best for your customer. And either way, if you sell someone something that is not a good fit for them, you can guarantee they will not come BACK to buy from you again. (The REAL money is made on the backend in business.)

And so, this ensures you are always doing what's *right*—and not what's *expedient*.

What's going to help your *customer*, and not necessarily just help *you*.

Plus, you won't even be tempted to use manipulation, bullying and conning.

Which leads us to the second reason why this is so important:

People Are ALWAYS
More Easily Persuaded
By People They *Trust*.

This is why it's so much easier for people who are the same age, race, profession, religion, etc., as their prospect to sell than someone who is not. (Crackerjack Selling Secret #41).

And if someone knows you have their best *interest* at heart, they will (almost) always at least give you a fair hearing, as they will likely trust you more than everyone else trying to sell them something.

This doesn't mean you will *always* make the sale.

But it does give you a huge advantage over those who obviously don't care.

Look, I KNOW this sounds simple and basic. But I can assure you, sincerely *caring* about someone before you try to sell them something will make the next 100 Crackerjack Selling secrets far more powerful. And by the way, when I say care, I don't mean caring about the *outcome* of whether or not they buy. (As you'll see in Crackerjack Selling Secret #7, that's a no-no.)

But as Ken McCarthy says in his book, *The System Club Letters*, when it comes to business:

*"He Who Cares Most
About People, Wins."*

Crackerjack Selling Secret #2:
The Dog Cookie Secret

This second Crackerjack Selling secret is also extremely powerful.

In fact, it is the essence of *all* persuasion.

Those who apply it often find selling to be extremely easy and even "routine." Something that comes naturally and quickly no matter what the product is.

I simply call it:

"The Dog Cookie Secret"

Probably the best demonstration I've seen of this was from Doug D'Anna.

Doug is a world-class direct mail copywriter (i.e. a "salesman in print"—who gets paid big bucks to persuade complete *strangers* to buy products and services they did not even know existed 5 minutes earlier via an ad or email). Anyway, I once had a conversation with him about his selling methods. And to illustrate how sales REALLY works, he asked if I have a dog. When I said yes, he asked, "does your dog come when you call her?"

"Sometimes, but she's pretty stubborn."

"I bet I can get her to come flying over to me, even though she doesn't know me."

"How?"

"All I have to do is hold up her favorite cookie. She'll come flying over to me. Am I right?"

He sure was.

You see, while I can spend hours trying to *manipulate* and *coax* my dog to come to me (like most sales and marketing people do to prospects when trying to get new business)—all I *really* have to do is hold up her favorite *cookie*.

Bernard Baruch—called "the most persuasive man of the 20th century"—put it like this:

"Find out what people want,
then show them how to get it."

You can spend a *fortune* on sales training and never see this fact brought forth so boldly and beautifully.

Bottom line?

If you want to sell more products and services, find what your prospects want more than anything else. Then show them how your product will give it to them. (Either as a *reward*—Crackerjack Selling Secret #49—or as a natural result of buying.)

Do that, and selling is *cake*.

Crackerjack Selling Secret #3:
Question Mark Mastery

Years ago, in high school, I knew a guy who *loved* debating people.

He had an uncanny way of taking a subject—*any* subject, even if he knew little or nothing about it—and debating others with more knowledge than himself and still win. It was truly incredible to watch him, for example, debate a guy who almost went pro in baseball about the subject, and make him look silly and *feeble* on the subject.

Question is, how did he do it?

How was he able to persuade experts on a subject to change their minds or conclusions when he knew sometimes nothing at all about that subject?

Years later, I realized how he did it:

He simply asked questions.

LOTS of questions. You see, there's an old saying (similar to the one we read at the end of Crackerjack Selling Secret #1) in sales that goes something like this:

> **"He Who Asks**
> **The Most Questions**
> **In Sales, Wins."**

And while that may not *always* be true, it certainly gives you a "leg up" whenever you want to persuade someone to buy something.

Why?

Because, when you ask questions, people will tell you *exactly* what they want to hear from you in order to sell them. It's almost like a teacher giving students the answers to an exam before taking it. Master salesmen—going all the way back to the senators and debaters of ancient Greece—have known this for *thousands* of years.

Unfortunately, much of today's sales training does not teach this.

Instead, it often involves springing a number of canned sales "closes" on people.

Yet, that is 100% the WORST thing you can do. In fact, as you will see in Crackerjack Selling Secret #29, when you want someone to buy, the best thing you can do is...

> **Shut Up!**

Ask a question and shut up.

Ask another question and shut up.

Ask another question and shut up.

If you ask the *right* questions—because, remember, you *care* about them and want to *help* them—eventually, you will have all the information you need in order to sell them (assuming it is a good fit for their situation, of course). They will tell you *everything* you need to know—what they want, how they want it and what they're willing to do (and *pay*) to get it.

Crackerjack Selling Secret #4:
Give Your Prospects "Buying Glasses"

Do you know who Jim Camp is?

Jim Camp is one of the most respected (and *feared*) negotiators on the planet.

His near-magical negotiating methods have been featured on **CNN, CNBC, The Wall Street Journal, Fortune, Harvard Business Review, Fast Company, Inc**., and more. Over 100,000 people have used his negotiation training and management system (in over 500 multi-national organizations) to complete *thousands* of business transactions totaling over $100 billion.

Anyway, one of his "big secrets" of *selling* people on his ideas is to simply...

Create *Vision*.

In fact, Jim brags about how he has never used a Powerpoint presentation.

And he pokes fun at many of the big name popular sales trainers with their fancy one-liners and tactic-based (as opposed to *principle*-based) methods. Instead of trying to wrestle prospects to the ground, and pound them with selling tactics and intellectual "brute force", Jim simply creates *vision*.

One example I heard Jim give was about seat belts.

Every day intelligent people die in car accidents because they don't wear seat belts. But what do you see all the seatbelt advocates do? They quote statistics about how millions of people die from not wearing seat belts and other intellectual and logical appeals. And yet, every year, thousands of smart people—who know the facts and statistics from school and the media—die in car accidents.

Clearly, appealing to the intellect isn't enough.

But, if you instead ask a question or make a statement that creates *vision* (such as, "where's your head going to end up if you slam on the breaks and you fly through the windshield at 75 mph?")...

**You Are FAR
More Likely to Sell
People on Wearing Seat Belts!**

Because now people can "see" it.

They can even *feel* themselves going through that windshield. As a result, they are more likely to put their seat belt on next time they get into their car—with no statistics or Powerpoint presentations required.

It's the same with your selling, too.

Let your prospects experience whatever you are trying to persuade them to do (or not do).

You'll see some specific ways to create vision throughout this book.

Stay tuned

Crackerjack Selling Secret #5:
Persuasion Secret of a Trial Lawyer Who Never Loses

Another one of my "persuasion heroes" is Gerry Spence.

Gerry Spence—love him or hate him—is probably THE best trial lawyer who has ever

lived. His courtroom "miracles" dwarf anything created by Hollywood or TV. And he has never lost a criminal trial in his life (and hasn't lost a civil trial since 1969).

In fact, he's so amazingly effective at what he does... the defense bar's leading once accused him of...

Hypnotizing the Jury!

Even to the point where he tried to get the judge to ban Gerry from using such "trickery" in the court.

All of which begs the question...

What really makes Gerry this all-fired persuasive?

According to his book, *How to Argue and Win Every Time*, the real magic behind his persuasive abilities has nothing to do with hypnosis, mind games or "tricks."

No, according to Gerry, it is simply...

Superior *Preparation*.

This is what separates the men from the boys in anything in life—law, politics, sports, academics and... yes... business and *sales*.

If you want to sell more products and services... and with much less *effort*... get to know as much about the person (or *people*—if you are selling to a large group) as possible. What are their likes? Their dislikes? What keeps them awake at night plagued with insomnia? What scares them? What are their political affiliations? What to do they do for fun? What do they do for a job? What TV shows do they watch? What magazines or books do they read?

These kinds of questions are important because they will help you discover that all-important piece of information we discussed earlier:

What Is The "Cookie"
They Want More
than Anything Else?

Doing this will go a LONG way towards making you a master seller.

Even if you lack the natural communication and selling skills of your competition.

21

Crackerjack Selling Secret #6:
Say Yes to No

This next Crackerjack Selling secret is almost counter-intuitive.

Especially if you have been indoctrinated in the "wrestle 'em to the ground and put 'em in a headlock until they say YES!" school of sales. And that is to always, Always, ALWAYS give prospects...

**Permission
To Say "No"**

Why would you do this?

Why go out of your way to tell them it's okay to tell you no?

Think of it like this, imagine two people trying to sell you a car. One of them comes up to you and starts using all the normal sales "tricks"—telling you how they have a great new car that just came in that day on accident (yeah, right!), how they have it saved just for you (uh-huh), how they were going to give it to the boss's nephew and so you better take it now... etc., etc., etc.

And the other salesman does the *opposite*: He simply asks you a few questions before anything else (Crackerjack Selling Secret #3), and says, "I think we may have what you're looking for. However, if it's not, will you just tell me no so we don't waste any of your time?"

In this case, which of the salesmen do you think *cares* (Crackerjack Selling Secret #1) most about you ?

Which one inspires more *trust*?

And, even more importantly...

**Which One Are You
More Likely
to Buy From?**

Anyway, here's the point:

When you are trying to sell someone something, if you rob them of their right to say "no" (by not giving them the option) he or she immediately goes on "defense"—and will automatically start thinking up ways to get away from you—both *emotionally* and *physically*.

If you want to sell like a pro, you have to *open* the other person's mind.

Not *shut* it.

Fact is, when you open peoples' minds, they are more likely to *sell themselves* (Crackerjack Selling Secret #79) and feel completely at ease with you—like they would around a friend. And there is no better way to open someone's mind to what you have to say than by telling them—right from the start—it's perfectly okay to tell you no.

Counter intuitive?

Yep.

And that's probably why so few people—even those who know about it—actually *do* it.

Crackerjack Selling Secret #7:
The "Nerd Gets Cheerleader" Phenomenon

Back in High School, there was an extremely "nerdy" guy—the women laughed at and the guys tortured and humiliated at every opportunity—who once got a date with one of the hottest girls in school.

The rest of the guys were in total *awe*.

People wondered, how did THIS guy get THAT kind of woman to go on a date with him? Plus, not only did she go on a date with him... but she practically *hounded* him wherever he went. She called him two or three times a day. Her friends thought she was crazy and nobody in the entire school could understand how this nerdy, pimple-popping guy was able to do this.

Then one day, one of the guys asked him what his "secret" was.

His answer:

"I stopped *caring* if girls told me no or not," he said. "I stopped taking it personally. So I asked her out as if I didn't care one way or the other if she said yes or no. A couple days later we went out." He continued, "Then, when I saw how well that worked, I kept doing it. When we talked on the phone, I would end the conversation half way through as if I didn't really care she was the prettiest and most popular girl in school. When we made out, I would sometimes stop just when she was getting into it and go home. And I just keep this attitude all the time now. She knows I don't really *need* her. It drives her crazy."

Amazing, isn't it?

Of course, this is nothing new. In sales, we call it...

Posture.

And top sales people have maximum posture ALL the time.

There is no argument when they're told no. No blubbering or begging. They simply have the attitude, "Okay, good luck" and remove themselves *emotionally* from the outcome.

And you know what?

When YOU have posture like this—where you don't care if they say yes or no—people feel an almost...

Irresistible Desire to
Comply with Your Wishes!

There's something magical that happens when people know you don't "need" their money. You don't "need" their deal. You don't "need" their contacts or whatever you are trying to persuade them to give you. If they don't say yes, someone else will and you don't care. Period.

Only question is, how do you develop this kind of iron-clad posture?

Especially when you really *do* want the sale and, in fact, really *do* need it?

The answer is to always have enough "irons in the fire" (i.e. deals going) so if one or two or three don't work, you really don't care. In my direct response copywriting business, for example, I have many people wanting to hire me. So I really don't care if someone says no or decides to flake out or whatever.

I mean, who cares?

And that's the key:

Use the secrets in this book to have so many prospects interested in buying,...

You Won't Care
If Someone Says No!

In fact, *you* may have to start telling other people no (Crackerjack Selling Secret #14). When this happens, believe me, people will practically *smell* your posture.

And in some cases, even people who would normally NOT buy will change their minds.

Crackerjack Selling Secret #8:
The "Ninja" Question

This secret is related to Crackerjack Selling Secret #3 (asking questions).

Except, in this case, you are asking questions with a "twist" to them.

A twist that helps you get to the heart of what someone *really* wants (Crackerjack Selling Secret #2). This is important because most of us may *think* we know what we want... only to discover later we were *wrong*. (Which is one reason why surveys and focus groups—while generally helpful—are not usually all that reliable.)

And one way to understand someone's REAL desire is to ask what I call the "ninja question."

For example, let's say you are a car salesman.

And someone comes to the lot and says, "I'm looking at getting a car that has..." and lists all the things she wants in a car. Most salesmen would probably show the customer exactly the kind of car she's looking for and try to match those cars up with as many of the details the customer described.

However, much more powerful than simply asking her what she wants is...

**Asking Her
What She Likes
about Her *Current* Car.**

This can make a HUGE difference.

Why?

Because often times, if you ask someone what they like about their previous car and their current car (and this goes with anything—I'm just using cars as an example) you will get *different* responses. Weird as it sounds, by asking someone what they currently like about what they have RIGHT NOW... you will find out what they REALLY want. And not just what they "say" (or think) they want.

Smart sales pros do this *all* the time.

Savvy real estate agents, for example, will ask "what do you like about your house now?" and then tailor their search around that FIRST—and what the customer *says* he wants second. This is a simple way to get deep inside someone's mind and sell without relying on "tricks."

Crackerjack Selling Secret #9:
Storytelling Magic

Remember **Cr**ackerjack Selling Secret #6—about creating *vision*?

Well, the following tip is one of the best ways to do so. In fact, it is easily one of the single most reliable ways to sell a product or service ever *invented.*

Why?

Because a brief story can pry open the most tightly-closed minds and even...

Change the Way
People Think!

Let me give you an example:

In his book *The Enemy Within*, conservative radio talk show host Michael Savage tells the story of his first job fresh out of college as a social worker. He was dead broke, living in a tiny apartment, and was sleeping on a mattress on the floor with two orange crates as lamp stands and no other furniture. And yet, the welfare clients he was helping got free beds, free coffee tables, free sofas, etc.—all the things most people have to work their fingers to the bone for—without working, and on the taxpayer's dime.

This short, simple story *perfectly* illustrated his point about how the system is flawed.

No complicated statistics or expensive government studies were needed to make his point.

That's the power of *stories*. They open closed minds. Let you "say" more with fewer words. And give people the chance to convince *themselves* your point is valid...

Without Lecturing, Arguing
Or Confrontation.

This is why stories are, have always been, and always *will* be the chief process by which human beings absorb and spread information.

We are literally "wired" at birth with a love of stories.

Some of the best sales pitches, negotiations, marketing campaigns and even courtroom arguments are centered around nothing more than a simple story.

And the best part is, you already know how to do it!

Just tell a story of customers who successfully used what you're selling, etc.

Yep... it really is that easy.

Crackerjack Selling Secret #10:
The Persuasion Proverb

Whether you're Christian or not, or even believe in God or not, you can learn a LOT of powerful selling methods in the Holy Bible.

One of which is in **Matthew 5:25**:

"Agree with thy adversary..."

While Jesus was talking about agreeing as a way of *protecting* yourself and your credibility, it is also true when you are selling.

Why?

Because, in the history of the world, nobody has ever "won" an argument. You may have all the facts, figures and "the truth*"* on your side... but that doesn't mean you "won" the argument. This is proven every U.S. presidential election. If you are a hardcore Republican, nothing you say will persuade a hardcore Democrat to vote for your candidate—and vice versa.

Plus, even if you do have all the facts in your favor, what will often happen is a little thing called:

"Cognitive Dissonance"

This is where someone continues believing something even after that belief has been *demolished*.

We are all vulnerable to this phenomena to some extent because we are all ego driven and hate being proved wrong. All of which means you will never persuade someone to do something—especially in sales—if you *argue*.

Frankly, that's the LAST thing you want to do.

It is far better to listen, *process* what they are saying, and then use it to your advantage... by asking more questions. In fact, if you refuse to argue and, instead, ask enough of the right *questions* (Crackerjack Selling Secret #3)—that build *vision* (Crackerjack Selling Secret #4) that are based on you sincerely *caring* about your customers (Crackerjack Selling Secret #1)—you will be surprised by how quickly people will come to their own conclusions to buy what you have.

Crackerjack Selling Secret #11:
How to win over skeptics

Do you know who Kevin Trudeau—the infomercial guy—is?

Mr. Trudeau is nothing if not *controversial*.

He's had his problems in the past with the government, has had LOADS of bad publicity, and a lot of people don't like him, much less *trust* him. Even so, his infomercials sell products like hotcakes. And one of the main reasons why is because he often *demonstrates* his products.

For example, his original "Natural Cures" infomercial used a short demonstration to sell *millions* of books...

Even To People
Who *Hated* Him!

Including one of my friends—who thought he was a con man.

Here's how Kevin did it:

Basically, he told the story (Crackerjack Selling Secret #9) about a friend of his with acid reflux. This is a common problem plaguing a LOT of people. And Kevin simply told the story of how his friend asked for his advice, and he told him to take a shot of vinegar. It happened to work like a charm for his friend—no more acid reflux.

After that (and before that) the rest of the infomercial was basically teasing and talking.

But Kevin gave a secret away in just this one part *demonstrating* his knowledge. And my friend (who thought Kevin was a shyster) did it because it was a problem she was having and figured she had nothing to lose.

Long story short, it worked for her and, in that one instant...

She Went from
Skeptic to *Believer*!

Now she's reading all his stuff all because he demonstrated that one *little* claim.

And that's why, many times if you *demonstrate* your product, you can often persuade people—even those with closed minds and who are *against* you now—to buy what you are selling.

Crackerjack Selling Secret #12:
Why Flaws are Your Friends

This is going to sound strange at first.

But if you hear me out, I think you will find admitting your product or service's "flaws" openly and forthrightly to be one of the most effective ways to sell you ever use.

One of the best examples of this was told by the late advertising genius David Ogilvy.

He was shopping for some furniture and came across something he wanted to buy. But before he could buy it, the sales man basically told him (and I'm paraphrasing here), "Look, I can't sell you this unless you see this huge scratch in the back..." David Ogilvy—who was in the often morally-challenged world of advertising, and used to seeing lies in selling—

Was Astonished!

Never in his life had a sales rep been that open and honest about a flaw.

And not only did he buy that piece of furniture... but he told all his friends about it and, I can only assume, sent that business many *more* customers.

Even more importantly:

David Ogilvy then made this principal of admitting flaws a *staple* of his advertising agency (the famous *Ogilvy & Mather* ad agency) which helped his agency sell far more products and services than most of his competitors.

But WHY does this work so well?

How come it doesn't actually result in LESS sales?

Probably because most people have never dealt with anyone—business or personal—who is 100% *straight* and honest with them. And so, when you become that person who is honest and ethical—even to the point of admitting a flaw in your product...

You Stick Out
Like A Sore Thumb!

And are instantly *trusted* over everyone else.

Plus, as we saw in Crackerjack Selling Secret #1—people buy when they *trust* you.

In fact, Drayton Bird—another advertising and marketing genius—said it best:

> *"The art of persuasion starts with saying something*
> *so clearly true that people believe what you say next."*

And there's no better way to do that than by admitting your product's flaws.

Crackerjack Selling Secret #13:
The Bumbler's Advantage

This is probably one of the most *unusual* Crackerjack Selling methods in this book.

And like the last secret (admitting flaws), it sounds almost *weird* at first.

You see, contrary to what many think, people are not always best persuaded by the "flashiest and dashiest" salesman or most perfectly polished pitch. In fact, the best sales pros, politicians, negotiators and persuaders are almost the exact *opposite* in some cases.

Take Ronald Reagan, for example.

He was called "The Great Communicator." Yet, how many times did he say something off kilter during his press conferences? How many times did he bumble and stumble? How many times did he make remarks or comments that made people question his professionalism and intelligence?

Nobody knows for sure, but many suspect he did that on *purpose*.

Why?

Because it made him more "real."

He didn't put himself on a pedestal and talk *down* to you—he talked to you like a *regular* person talks to another *regular* person. And, as a result...

People LOVED
Him for It!

But Ronald Reagan wasn't the only one to do this.

Everyone from TV characters like "Columbo" to those dusty-looking (but extremely *successful*) vacuum cleaner salesmen who walk around in 20-year old suits and bad haircuts do this exact same thing.

Sometimes it's an act, of course.

But many times they just let themselves be who they are—*human*.

I have heard this concept referred to as being "un-okay." And if you think about it, we are ALL un-okay. We are all a bit unsure of ourselves. And by letting this shine through, we make ourselves "approachable." People feel they can open up and let us in their world.

And that's why, if you want to give yourself a leg up in sales, be a little "un-okay."

Let the other person feel as if they are in control and not look at you as a threat. Doing this means they'll open up to you and give you the information you need to sell them.

It's ironic, but being *boldly imperfect* in selling actually gives you an *advantage*.

Crackerjack Selling Secret #14:
Pull the Rug Out

When it comes to selling, there are few things more powerful than the "take away."

This is when you literally tell someone they *cannot* buy your product. Such as telling them that house is no longer for sale. Or saying 5 of your widgets are available and everyone else has to go on a waiting list. Or by stating something may not fit for them and they should look for a different product instead.

And so on and so forth.

This is related in many ways to Crackerjack Selling Secret #7—posture. Except, not only are you letting people know you do not *care* if they buy from you, but they cannot buy it even if they *wanted* to anyway.

One direct marketing expert I know (Ken McCarthy) put it like this:

You're painting a picture of heaven... in 3D technicolor and 360-degree Dolby surround sound... letting them linger in it until they own it, then...

**Pulling the Rug
Out From Under Them!**

Such as by placing an *obstacle* in the way of buying.

Or by telling them they can't have your product.

Or any other means you can realistically and *honestly* use to "take it away" you can think of.

This is powerful stuff. And once you start using it, and really don't *care* if the other person buys or not, you'll never look at selling the same. All the sudden the tables turn and, instead of you trying to sell to your customers...

**They Are Trying
to Sell You on
Letting Them Buy!**

Again, the best sales pros have been using the take away for centuries. They walk away from deals, tell the prospect they don't qualify, and a whole host of other things.

Do this in YOUR business and watch your sales go up automatically.

Crackerjack Selling Secret #15:
Take an Axe to Your Expert Status

Before I tell you about this next secret, a word of warning:

Some people—especially those who really are "experts" in a certain thing—*hate* hearing what I am about to say. I admit, I don't like it, either.

But like it or not, we are in what publicity expert Paul Hartunian calls a...

"Celebrity-Obsessed Culture"

What does that mean?

Simply this: People give FAR more attention, money and power to "celebrities" than they do "experts." This is why you can have scientists, doctors and other highly trained professionals' opinions trumped by some clueless Hollywood celebrity who decides to write a book on whatever "cause-of-the-month" they cling to.

For some reason, nobody cares so much what "experts" think about anymore...

Unless You
Are a *Celebrity*.

Which sucks if you're a "for real" expert trying to be heard.

But here's the good news:

This also means nearly anyone else—from your local grocer to a stay-at-home-mom—can make themselves "instant experts" just by making *themselves* celebrities. And to do that, simply get yourself featured by the media—radio, TV or print. Once you get on the radio, on the TV or in the newspapers, you automatically become an instant celebrity—with the media's *implied* endorsement.

I'll give you a "real life" example:

A couple years ago I wrote a book about dogs. And even though I have zero formal dog training or veterinary experience, when I was on the radio, listeners considered me an expert for no other reason than I was on the radio being interviewed and their local vet and dog trainer wasn't.

See how that works?

If you want to instantly sell more products and services, just get yourself in the media. Once a media outlet (no matter how small) "knights" you an expert, you will have a LOT more selling power on the topic you were interviewed about.

It's called the "halo effect."

People believe what they read in their favorite newspaper, hear on their favorite radio station, or see on their favorite TV news program. This is why you can spend years trying to persuade your own spouse to go in for a regular physical... only to have him or her spontaneously go after watching Oprah or Dr. Oz suggest it.

It's not that Oprah and Dr. Oz are any "smarter" than you.

**They Are Just
the Ones on TV!**

And the beauty of this is it's *easy*.

You simply send a press release to your local (or national) media. You can either do it yourself, or hire someone to do it for you (freelance journalists or journalism students at a good college are great for hiring to do this.)

Once the media runs a story about you, you become an *authority* on that topic. Everyone automatically believes you. They *trust* what you say. And, most importantly...

**They Buy Your
Products and Services!**

Bottom line? Use the power of the media, and watch your sales *soar*.

Crackerjack Selling Secret #16:
How to "Butter Up" Your Prospects to Buy

Believe it or not, much of sales comes down to timing.

By that I mean, offering someone the right *thing*, at the right *time*, and in the right *way*. If you want to position yourself in the best possible way to sell (Crackerjack Selling Secret #22), then make sure you get your timing right.

And guess what?

The best "time" for selling is BEFORE you want to sell someone something by giving them value, first.

Let me give you an example I once heard Gary Bencivenga (one of the world's top marketing geniuses) give to drive the point home. This has to do with door-to-door sales (probably the *hardest* kind of selling there is). But the idea can be applied to just about anything else. Back in the old days, certain door-to-door salesmen would get around the usual customer rejection (and *hostility*) by showing up and not necessarily trying to "sell" anything.

Instead they would show up with their ONLY agenda being to...

Give A Free *Sample*.

Then, maybe the next week they'd drop by again and give another little gift.

Again, nothing for sale.

No pressure.

And no "sales speak."

They may even have done this over and over again for *weeks*. And when that salesman—who at that point was highly *trusted* (Crackerjack Selling Secret #1) and even *welcomed*—finally did spring a sales pitch, it was not only *tolerated*... but many times *acted* upon.

There are some very powerful natural "laws" at work doing this.

The most important being the "law or reciprocity" (Crackerjack Selling Secret #81)—which essentially says: *"If you do something nice for someone, they feel an almost overwhelming urge to return the favor."* In this case, that "favor" is buying your products.

However, this phenomenon only works when you give value FIRST.

When you do that, you automatically position yourself in a way where your prospects are...

**Almost *Forced* to
at Least Hear You Out.**

And like many of the secrets in this book, this can apply to any type of selling, too.

In direct marketing, it's rare to sell to anyone "cold." Usually a free report, video or some kind of gift is given *before* asking for a sale. There is a smart salesman I know of who, as soon as you say something nice about him or thank him for his help, will often then ask you for referrals right on the spot. (When you're most likely to give one.) There have also been cases where someone who just wanted a raise at their job would "butter" their bosses up for weeks by bringing them doughnuts and food on Fridays—giving that value *first*, before asking for the sale.

Anyway, here's the point:

The best time to start selling is before you want to sell someone something.

It may sound strange, but it works like crazy.

Crackerjack Selling Secret #17:
One Way Cults Get You in the Door

If you are in the copywriting and/or direct marketing world, then chances are you have heard about the late, great marketing "wizard" Eugene Schwartz.

He was easily one of the most effective copywriters who ever lived.

His book *Breakthrough Advertising* is like a "bible" for serious copywriters. And my own copy is marked up and beaten to a pulp after some 15+ readings. Anyway, one of Schwartz's big selling secrets was what he called:

"Gradualization"

This simply means starting with facts your readers already believe... and then *logically* and *gradually* leading them to your more unbelievable facts. You will see certain religions and even *cult* movements doing this all the time. (I once was approached by a guy in a certain religion who did this with incredible precision—I didn't even know what he was up to at first, even though I STUDY persuasion all the time!)

You also see it used to sell products and services most people are pre-disposed to *reject*.

For example:

I heard this story of someone who does this in MLM. If he's talking to someone who is "cold", he never, EVER starts by saying he's in "MLM" or network marketing. Instead, he talks about how unstable the economy and job market is. Then he discusses how pensions and government programs are unreliable and bankrupt. Next he suggests real financial security comes only from having a business. And if you lack experience, a franchise is ideal, since they usually offer support and a proven "paint by numbers" *system*. But franchises cost money and take time. So the next best thing is MLM—which can be done cheaply part time. And since most new MLM company's fail, it's best to join one that's been around a while, like his...

See how that works?

He doesn't say anything about "MLM" (most people run when they hear the word) until they've been *prepared* to hear it first.

It's a brilliant way to sell something people might normally outright reject.

And you can just as easily use it for any kind of selling situation (especially if you are selling to skeptics). Just start with what your prospects *already* believe and accept, and move one step at a time towards your product.

Crackerjack Selling Secret #18:
How to be a Sales "Stud"

In some ways, this is probably the most *powerful* sales method in this book.

In fact, it is so powerful... and works so reliably and *consistently*... it may be the ONLY method you really need. What I'm talking about is...

"Social Proof"

This term was coined (as far as I can tell) by the brilliant social psychologist Robert Cialdini in his book *Influence: The Psychology of Persuasion*. It basically means people will do (and buy) things they see other people are doing (and buying)—especially people they know, trust or can relate to.

In other words, if you show your prospects how *other* people (especially if it's people your prospects *respect*) are using *your* product or service...

They Will Be Much More
Likely to Buy from You, Too!

Clothing and food businesses do this all the time.

For example, if Johnny All-Star Athlete is wearing a certain brand of shoes, then you can be sure his *fans* are wearing them. Even if they find those shoes uncomfortable or ugly. If Joe Movie Star eats at a specific restaurant, then you can be sure many of his *fans* will be eating there, too. Even if they find the food stale and the service substandard. If Jane Politician is wearing a certain kind of glasses frame, then you can be sure many of her *fans* will be buying those frames. Even if the style doesn't fit their looks and even if they don't need glasses. (We all saw this when Sarah Palin hit the national stage during the 2008 presidential election—there was a *huge* run on her exact glasses frames.)

And so on, and so forth.

Frankly, you can get contacts, sales or even just an appointment with someone, simply by showing the person you know his or her friends or colleagues.

Which is why, one of the FIRST things I look for is social proof when selling.

If I can say one of the market's authority figures is using the product, then there's a good chance people will buy what I'm selling...

Sight Unseen!

Social proof is easily one of the most powerful selling "tools" you can possess.

And the best part is, it takes zero effort to use.

Crackerjack Selling Secret #19:
How to Sell to Complete Strangers

Do you want to know the secret of instantly "bonding" with someone so they trust you?

Even a complete stranger?

Then find a common "enemy" with your prospects. Doing this is like turning up your "sales temperature" 50 degrees (or more)...

Right Out the Gate!

It's absolutely true... and I'm going to *prove* it to you right now.

Let's say you sell to a market dominated by hard core pro-life Christians (of which I am a part). And let's say you want to "break the ice" in that new market with an ad you're writing, a speech you're giving, or even if you are in their living room doing a face-to-face sales presentation. One of the *easiest* ways to become more trusted and "liked" is to simply let it be known (assuming it's true—if you lie, it WILL backfire on you) how much you can't stand the pro-choice, anti-religion politician always making headlines in the local news.

I'm not saying to be in anyone's face about it, or to force the issue.

Just a passing joke, reference or comment will, in many cases, do the trick.

You will see this done all the time in, for example, direct mail ads for investing or on news sites like NewsMax.com or WorldNetDaily.com. This is not a sales "tactic" or "trick" if you really do *believe* what you say. All you are doing is establishing a bond—a shared *connection*—with your prospects. When you have a common enemy—and it's *real*, not bogus—with someone, that person will like and trust you much more than if you don't share that feeling.

And people are always more likely to buy from those...

They *Like* and *Trust*.

This goes back to *preparation*—really knowing your customer. (Crackerjack Selling Secret #5.)

And is one of those things where one or two "choice words" can make or break the sale.

Crackerjack Selling Secret #20:
The Veterinarian's Sales Trick

Back when I was writing my book about dogs, I learned how to get a dog to behave at the vet's office.

What you do is, you take your dog to the vet *before* making an appointment for any services. Reason why is your dog can meet the vet with no anxiety, shots or pain associated with the trip. Instead, the ONLY purpose of the visit is to...

Make A New *Friend*.

That way, the next time you take your dog to the vet, he/she will be way more relaxed and associate the vet office's smells and sounds in a *good* way—as a friendly place to be *visited*, instead of a painful and anxious place to be *avoided*.

Well guess what?

It's the same with us humans. If you want to sell someone something, make a friend *first*...

Before You Start
Any Selling.

Why?

Because just like with our furry dog friends, we are much more likely to hear our friends out. As well as *believe* our friends have our best interests at heart. This is done in the direct marketing world all the time. Many of the best selling ads don't spring a sales pitch on you. They befriend you first (by doing things like establishing a *common enemy*, for example). This way they get to know you and let you get to know them.

Bottom line?

We are ALL much more likely to buy from a friend—someone we know, like and trust—than a complete stranger. Which is why if you want to increase your sales and close more deals, make a friend before you try to make a sale.

Crackerjack Selling Secret #21:
Turn Off the Pressure

Let's face it: People *hate* being pressed into making decisions.

Frankly, we *resent* it.

And that's why, if you put a bunch of pressure on someone to do something—such as when you are selling—you might as well call them a dirty name while you're at it. Because whatever it is you want them to do just ain't going to happen.

That's why, whenever you are selling—big or small—it is far better to...

**Put the Person
At *Ease*.**

Remove the pressure ANY way you can.

Whether you're trying to sell to a room of people, writing an ad, or doing "full contact" sales one-on-one—pretend you are talking to them over a frosty beverage or drink at a cozy bar. Relaxed. Laid back. No pressure either way—whether they agree to what you want or not. **(**See Crackerjack Selling Secret #7**.)** This also ties into Crackerjack Selling Secret # 6—giving permission to say "no." The more relaxed and "unguarded" your prospect is, the more likely he or she is to buy from you.

Always remember:

If you want sell to more, remove ALL the pressure. It hardly ever works and, in fact, usually turns people *off.*

Crackerjack Selling Secret #22:
The Cereal Box Phenomenon

Ever notice how the highest selling products are rarely ever the best tasting, best quality or best priced?

Take cereal for example.

There are certain brands of cereal that sell like hot cakes... even though they taste horrible, are *devoid* of nutrition, and are almost *twice* as expensive as their competitors.

How do they do it? What's their "secret"?

Positioning.

Smart food manufacturers fight tooth and nail to have their stuff at "eye level" on the shelf.

Doing so almost guarantees their product gets seen, noticed and *bought* before any other products. (Even if their competition offers a better product at a better price.)

And guess what?

You can use this exact same principle to make selling a breeze. In fact, positioning is THE key to easy sales. It controls what people *think* about you. It controls how people *feel* about you. And it even controls what other people *say* about you.

All of which is why, the better your positioning is...

The *Easier* Selling Is!

And if you simply position yourself as the "top dog" in your industry or niche, you will be in the all-coveted "cat bird seat" (Crackerjack Selling Secret #98)—the position to which a ton of new business and money flow freely. Examples would be Perry Marshall (in the Google AdWords niche). Ken McCarthy (in the Internet marketing niche). Zig Ziglar (in the sales niche). Jay Abraham (in the direct marketing world). Amazon.com (in online book sellers). Kleenex (lots of people say, "I want a Kleenex" instead of "I want a tissue".)

And the list goes on.

These people and businesses have "top of mind status" in their respective industries.

And, frankly, even if they decided to start offering shoddy products and treated their customers like slime, they would STILL automatically attract large sums of money. (For a while, at least.) And it's all because of their positioning—the most valuable asset they could have.

Best part?

No need to rack your brains trying to position yourself if you use the secrets in this book.

In fact, when you use Crackerjack Selling, good positioning happens *automatically*.

(And by the way... If you don't know where to start, then simply position yourself as the one person who stands against fraud in your industry. This instantly positions you as a trusted expert in your niche.)

Crackerjack Selling Secret #23:
How Columbo Did It

Ever watch that TV show "Columbo"?

It starred Peter Falk as Lieutenant Columbo, an LA Police Department homicide detective. And one of Columbo's "trademark" methods for getting the bad guys was to talk with them, make it look like he wasn't suspicious anymore, and... right before walking out the door (when the villain's "guard" was down) say, "... by the way..." and then...

**Ask the REAL Question
That'd Give the Villain Away!**

And guess what?

You can do the same thing to get to the heart of your customers' and prospects' REAL problems—that maybe they don't want to admit (for any number of reasons). It all goes back to <u>Crackerjack Selling Secrets #'s 2</u> and <u>3</u>—finding out what someone REALLY wants (either as something *desired* or a problem they need *solved*) and then asking questions. If you aren't getting anywhere with asking questions (many times people *cling* to their pain, and are reluctant to talk about it), a simple Columbo moment often gets the job done. In other words, you finish with your questions and end the conversation or make like you will be changing the subject.

As a natural result, the other person will usually let their "guard" down.

At that point, you say...

"By the Way..."

And then ask another—more *probing*—question. (<u>Crackerjack Selling Secret #65</u>**.**)

It may sound simple (and it is), but it's also extremely effective.

I also have to stress, if you have your head on straight with actually *caring* about someone you want to sell to first (<u>Crackerjack Selling Secret #1</u>), then this is a *natural* extension of wanting to help them. As you've seen, many of the secrets in this book are principle-based. But this one is obviously more tactic-based. And so, I want to warn you not to look at this as a way to "manipulate." If you do, it will backfire on you (people can sense when they are being manipulated.)

True, when Columbo used it, he was being manipulative in a sense.

But when you use it in business to sell or market—and this goes for any tactic-based secret you read in this book—you do NOT want to use it for that purpose.

The purpose of it is to get to the heart of the real problems that need solving. To help your customer by asking the right questions and probing. (Frankly, you may find your product is not a right "fit" for them and could very well not even be good for them at all. Again, the customer comes *first*.)

So always remember:

If you use any of these secrets to manipulate your customers—instead of to *help* them solve an urgent problem in their lives—you will (rightfully) crash and burn.

Crackerjack Selling Secret #24:
Benjamin Franklin on Steroids

One of the most diplomatic and *successful* Americans who ever lived was Benjamin Franklin.

Not only was he one of America's first self-made millionaires, but he was known for being able to get an awful lot accomplished (diplomatically) overseas during times of high tension in the early days of the American Republic.

What was his "secret"?

He Refused to Say Anything
Bad About People.

When others gossiped about someone, Benjamin Franklin found something *nice* to say.

In fact, his "rule of thumb" was never say anything about someone behind their back you wouldn't say to their face. As a result, he was always listened to, his ideas were often considered, and, at the end of the day, he was...

Extremely Persuasive in
Business, Sales and Politics!

People instinctively distrust gossipers.

And we avoid and ignore those who routinely ridicule people behind their backs.

After all, if person A is always making fun of or tearing down person B behind his back, then what's he saying about you behind *yours*? If he's complaining about his customers over *there*... what's he saying about his customers over *here*? Such activities make selling extremely hard by erasing that bridge of trust needed to make a sale. (Crackerjack Selling Secret #1.)

Which is why, not only should you NOT gossip about others... but you should try to engage in what I call...

"Reverse Gossip"

Here's what I mean:

Whenever someone is NOT around, and cannot hear what you are saying, *praise* them to the moon. Tell others about why someone (or group of people) are so great. Say good things—especially things that would make those you are talking about blush if they heard it.

This makes you A.) more trust-worthy and B.) MUCH more persuasive.

People WANT to be around and associated with others who engage in reverse gossip. And, later on when you want to sell to those who hear your reverse gossip, they will be more receptive.

The only "catch" to this is you must be *sincere*.

Don't kiss butt and don't lie.

Find something you *genuinely* believe about other people and start with that.

If you do this for 30 days, I think you will be shocked at the results.

Crackerjack Selling Secret #25:
7 Words That Force "Hemmers & Hawers" off the Fence

I first heard about the following from negotiation "wizard" Jim Camp.

It is a very powerful way to persuade someone to make a "yes or no" decision when selling or negotiating. And it also happens to be very *easy* to do.

Anyway, here is what you do:

Pretend you are trying to sell your product or service to a customer who is on the "fence." For whatever reason, he can't make up his mind and is "hemming and hawing" making a decision. Or, even worse, is on the verge of not making a decision at all (which, as you know, basically means, "no.") You've given your sales pitch, answered all his questions, and now there's silence.

What do you do?

Well, a lot of sales books and trainings say to shut up—as he or she who talks next "loses." However, instead of remaining silent in this situation, I would suggest just asking this:

**"What Do You
Want Me to Do?"**

This question *forces* a yes or no answer.

You're not asking them to "do" anything other than to tell you what to do. You are giving them the ultimate *power* to decide, taking away the pressure (Crackerjack Selling Secret #21) and giving them the *authority* to tell you "no" (Crackerjack Selling Secret # 6). The result, in many cases, is a decision of yes or no (or they give up some more useful information for you.)

And in either case...

You Win!

Because if they tell you to go away, and they aren't interested, great! You can move on and stop wasting time with them. On the other hand, they may tell you to ring up the order right there on the spot. Or, at the very least, give some more information that leads to the sale.

The key here is not to persuade them to *buy*... but to just make a *decision*.

The former pressures people and pushes them away.

The latter gives them the power, takes away the pressure and puts the responsibility on them.

Crackerjack Selling Secret #26:
Sing the Socrates Song

If you've ever read the book *How to Win Friends and Influence People* then you likely have seen "The Socrates Method."

The "Socrates Method" (as Dale Carnegie called it) is definitely tactical (so use with caution—and in strict accordance with Crackerjack Selling Secret #1: Sincerely *caring* about people.) But it is also a subtle way of persuading people to buy from you. (In any form—verbal, written, video, audio, etc).

Here's how it works:

Amongst other things… Socrates was known as the greatest master of *persuasion* who ever lived. He was especially famous for being a world-class debater who converted even his bitterest *opponents*—who passionately *disagreed* with him—to his side of an argument. One of his secrets was to simply get the other person to keep saying the word "yes" over and over during the conversation by asking questions people would have to agree with. And he kept asking these "yes" questions (Crackerjack Selling Secret #3) again and again and again… until he racked up a pile of them.

And do you know what would happen?

Nine out of 10 times his opponents would eventually find themselves agreeing with him…

Even Though They Were 100%
Dead-Set *Against* Him
At the Start of the Debate!

I've used this for everything from politics to sports and it really does work.

And you may be surprised how many hard-core sales people (especially the "door-to-door" types) use this sleepy method when selling. In fact, if you call *Encyclopedia Britannica* and tell them you're interested in possibly buying a set of their encyclopedias, I have been told (and this was many years ago, and may have changed) the sales rep will immediately begin to use this method. World-class sales trainer Brian Tracy once said that every time you get your customers to say "yes"… you raise the chances of them buying from you another "degree" or two. The more they say "yes" the better the chances of them saying "yes" when you ask for the sale.

Anyway, try it and see what happens.

You'll quickly realize this isn't just a bunch of dorky philosophical mumbo-jumbo.

And, in fact, does get people almost in a *habit* of saying yes to you as long as you are talking about something they already want (Crackerjack Selling Secret #2).

Crackerjack Selling Secret #27:
Speak Thou in Parables

Believe it or not, one of the greatest salesmen in history was Jesus Christ.

If you go by total numbers, longevity and influence—He would have to be #1. His "Book" is the most published in history. Untold *billions* of dollars have been donated to His cause. And His "brand" has been around—and *thriving*—for over 2,000 years.

Can any other business or historical figure match that?

And one of His best—and *easiest* to use—sales secrets was to...

Speak in *Parables*.

A parable is a fictional story or event used to illustrate what you want to say.

And, when it comes to selling, it is very, very powerful (and related to Crackerjack Selling Secret #9—telling stories.) One of my favorite examples can be found in chapter 3 of Joe Vitale's excellent book, *The 7 Lost Secrets of Success,* where he reprints a 1951 private memo from advertising genius **Bruce Barton**:

> *"Jesus told His listeners stories. The story, 'A certain man went down from Jerusalem to Jericho and fell among thieves.' Every one of His listeners knew some man who had fallen among thieves on that dangerous Jerusalem turnpike. They listened to the story and remembered it. If He had said, 'I want to talk to you about why you should be a good neighbor,' nobody would have listened."*

This is potent stuff once you understand it.

Simple parables have been used to sell *billions* of dollars worth of products and services—from MLM opportunities... to political candidates (dig up some old Ronald Reagan speeches for examples)... to even the *Wall-Street Journal*—which sold some $2 billion dollars worth of subscriptions at least partially based on the strength of an ad that starts out:

> *On a beautiful late spring afternoon, twenty-five years ago, two young men graduated from the same college. They were very much alike, these two young men. Both had been better than average students, both were personable and both—as young college graduates are—were filled with ambitious dreams for the future.*
>
> *Recently, these men returned to their college for their 25th reunion.*
>
> *They were very much alike. Both were happily married. Both had three children. And both, it turned out, had gone to work for the same Midwestern manufacturing company, and were still there.*
> *But there was a difference. One of the men was manager of a small department of that company. The other was its president.*

See the impact of a simple parable?

Use them and you will sell more—guaranteed.

Crackerjack Selling Secret #28:
The Power of a Solid

As a direct response copywriter, I study and collect a LOT of advertisements.

But not just any old ads. I study the ones that have been *tested, tracked* and *proven* to make the most money and sales. And one of the most reliable direct marketing selling methods I've ever seen is what some call...

"I need your help!"

Basically, what this means is, you ask someone to do something extremely *easy* for you... and in exchange you'll do something far MORE *valuable* for them. In the advertising world, this often means giving someone a free book, DVD or other valuable product in exchange for trying out a risk-free trial of a newsletter, health supplement or some other kind of continuity product. In fact, Boardroom Books—one of the biggest direct mailers in the world—made a fortune giving away free books and gifts in exchange for trying 6 free issues of their newsletter.

You can use this secret in your selling, too.

Whatever your situation, think of something valuable to do for your prospects in exchange for doing something easy for you.

Let your mind come up with all kinds of ideas, write them down, then go and test them on some people in your market. If you are doing direct marketing (and can't go out and ask your prospects in big numbers) email a list of things you can give away to people in your market and ask, "which of these appeals to you most?"

Of course, like all the secrets in this book, your results will be amplified 100-fold if you follow Crackerjack Selling Secret #2 (find out what they want), first.

And once you know what that "thing" they want is, find a way to give it to them in exchange for hearing you out or buying something from you.

Crackerjack Selling Secret #29:
Shutty

I don't watch a whole lot of TV.

But one show I love watching (now in re-runs) is called: *King of Queens*. And the main character, Doug, has a saying anyone in the selling should learn, know and memorize:

"Shutty!"

In other words, *shut up*.

The irony of selling is the majority of it should actually done "by" the person or people you are selling to—not by you. Ask any truly great salesman and they'll tell you there's a LOT of power in silence. One of the best demonstrations of this was actually on the old *Johnny Carson Show* (from back in the 1980's). I didn't get to see it when it happened (I was just a kid at the time). But I have heard several different sales and persuasion experts explain it like this:

Basically, Fred Herman—the "world's greatest salesman"—was a guest on Carson.

After a little banter, Johnny put Fred on the spot and basically said, "Okay Fred, you're supposed to be the world's greatest salesman. Sell me something!"

After a little back and forth, Johnny told Fred to sell him the ashtray on his desk.

Picking the ashtray up, Fred noticed an ash forming on Carson's cigarette (people used to smoke on late night shows back then). "Why would you want an ash tray like this, Johnny?" asked Fred (notice, he started with Crackerjack Selling Secret #3—asking *questions*.)

And Johnny proceeded to give Fred a detailed answer.

When he finished, Fred asked another (more important) question to get the REAL reason (Note: As any great salesman knows, the first reason, objection or excuse is NEVER the "real" reason)—Crackerjack Selling Secret #35). And the that question was: "Is that the only reason why?"

So, Johnny went on to another reason—an even more emotional and *important* one to him.

"That sounds like an important reason, Johnny."

"Yes, it is."

"What would you pay for this?"

"Five cents."

"Sold!"

Okay, tongue-in-cheek stuff aside, did you notice what happened?

Johnny Carson
Sold *Himself* the Ashtray!

Fred didn't really "do" anything except ask a couple questions and shut up and listen.

In the end, Johnny sold himself and the rest is history.

Now, whether that was a scripted skit (it probably was) or not isn't the point. The idea is to ask questions and then shut up and listen. And keep doing this the entire time you are talking with your prospect. As the late marketing "guru" Gene Schwartz said, *"Talk little, listen much."* If you ask questions and then shut up and listen, you can often make the sale by letting the prospect sell *themselves* on the reasons they would want your product. (This is especially true if you are trying to sell over the phone—that "mute" button on your phone can sometimes make the sales for you!)

Try it the next time you are selling someone something.

I think you'll find it works like a charm.

Crackerjack Selling Secret #30:
Watch Your Waiter

Back when I was slugging it out as an MLM distributor, trying to sell my friends, family and everyone within 3 feet of my opportunity, I got an incredibly useful piece of advice about persistence from an old sales guru.

Basically, what he said was: *"The key to selling is persistence."*

But, he said, the key to persistence is NOT to be in someone's face every five minutes—hovering over them like a mosquito looking for a tender area on their neck.

Instead, he said to...

Be Like a Good *Waiter*.

In other words, to notice how good waiters are *persistent*... yet not *annoying*.

He said to notice how the best waiters don't stop at your table every three minutes to bug you—but show up maybe every 10-20 minutes, fill up your drink and just check in when they see a gap in your dinner conversation (so as not to interrupt). The highest paid waiters—who get the most tips—do this all the time.

That, he said, is what sales follow-up is really about.

Not annoying anyone or clinging to them like white on rice. But to instead "check in" with every now and then—and always with some deed or idea to share...

That Brings *Value*
to Their Lives.

And not just an endless string of annoying sales pitches.

That's incredibly good advice back then, and it is even MORE important now. If you are trying to sell someone something—in person, on the phone or even in an email auto-responder sequence— be like a good waiter:

Persist—but never *annoy*.

Crackerjack Selling Secret #31:
Walk Like a Con Man

A couple chapters ago, I mentioned a funny TV show called *King of Queens*.

In this chapter, I have another show to tell you about. One with an equally powerful sales secret "embedded" in some of the episodes that is well worth watching for that reason. This other TV show is called "Lost." It's about the survivors of a plane crash on a bizarre island in the middle of the ocean. And each episode basically centers on the current predicament they are in... while showing flashbacks (and also flash forwards) of the character they are focusing on for that episode.

Anyway, one of the characters' names is "Sawyer."

And back in civilization he was a con man—AKA:

"A Confidence Man"

A guy who cons people—in his case, rich married women—out of their loot and runs.

And what Sawyer did in one episode was set up a fake business investment, pitch it to a rich woman's husband, and then threaten to walk away from the deal when the husband started getting skeptical. As expected, this further made the husband want to get in on the deal because Sawyer wasn't afraid to walk away—and even seemed *anxious* to (Crackerjack Selling Secret #7).

Now, my point here isn't to con people, obviously.

There is actually a powerful (and ethical) sales lesson here. And that is...

Tough Sales Pros Don't Fear
Walking Away from Deals!

No matter how big or important—if you are not afraid to walk away if things aren't going your way, you will be far more persuasive.

In fact, some of the toughest negotiators and sales pros on the planet do this as a matter of *routine*: Simply walk away if the deal doesn't go their way. Sometimes—and this goes back to posture (Crackerjack Selling Secret #7)—the other party changes their mind and agrees to the deal.

I once did this while buying a car.

They kept trying to get me to pay more than I was willing to pay. Finally, I just said, "This isn't going to happen unless you bring the price down. I appreciate your time. But I am going to check some other dealers out." You should have seen how *fast* these financing guys were to figure out a way to give me a better deal!

Anyway, walking away is like the takeaway (Crackerjack Selling Secret #14) on *steroids*.

It gives you a very powerful psychological advantage in any kind of selling.

Try it in your next sales or negotiation and you'll see exactly why.

Crackerjack Selling Secret #32:
The Harvard School of Easy Sales

This next Crackerjack Selling tip is so simple, most people miss it.

But if you give it a shot, I think you will find it not only works... but works so *reliably* and *consistently* it's almost spooky.

Check this out:

Many years ago, a study was done by a Harvard psychologist named Ellen Langer to illustrate a psychological principal that says when if we simply give a "reason" for why we want someone to do something for us, they will be much more likely to comply. She proved her case by going to a library to a line of people waiting to use the Xerox machine. When she asked people if she could cut in line, only 60% of people agreed. But when she gave a *reason* to let her cut in line (*"can I use the machine first, I'm in a rush?"*)...

A Whopping 94%
Of People Said "Yes"!

You can read more about this fascinating study in Robert Cialdini's book *Influence: The Psychology Of Persuasion.*

And guess what?

Smart marketers, sales professionals and negotiators do this ALL the time. In fact, one of the cornerstones of direct response marketing is called "reason why selling." This is why you never see successful businesses having just a regular sale.

No...

There Is Always
A REASON
For the Sale.

Maybe they ordered too many coats and so are giving them away at a discount.

Or there was a fire in the warehouse and some of the DVD player boxes got burnt (but the actual DVD players are fine) and so they are giving them away cheap.

Or they are going out of business and need to liquidate everything.

And so on and so forth.

I know of one successful furniture store that had so much success with these "damaged goods" type sales, the owner *purposely* poked holes in the roof of his warehouse so there really WOULD be small water damage on some of his furniture. Why? Because it gave him...

The Perfect "Excuse"

For His Sales!

And helped him sell FAR more of his wares than normal.

Anyway, the point is, whenever you are selling, try to think of a good "reason why" for your offer. Or why they must order right *now*. Or why there will never be a better time to buy, etc.

It seems so innocent and small.

But it works like *crazy*.

Crackerjack Selling Secret #33:
Beef Up Your "Sales Vibes"

Ever hear that "Beach Boys" song *Good Vibrations*?

Believe it or not, it contains a powerful Crackerjack Selling Secret that often works extremely well (even though it has nothing to do with "sales").

Let me explain:

One of my favorite all-time books is *The Boron Letters* by the late (great) marketing genius Gary Halbert. Gary was briefly in a federal prison for a crime that, in a moral sense, never even happened. (It had to do with some shady partners he was in business with not fulfilling orders, and the feds went after Gary since he was the easier target.) And while Gary was in jail (Boron Federal Prison), he wrote a series of 25 letters to his 16-year old son teaching him about the art and science of direct marketing (thus the name "Boron Letters".)

I absolutely *love* this book.

It is all "meat" and goes right for the *jugular* when it comes to marketing, selling, persuasion and everything in between.

Anyway, one of the pieces of advice he gave his son was to...

Hit the Weights!

His reason was, people who are in shape and strong, give off a "vibe" that scares bullies, con artists and other scum away. On the other hand, those who look weak actually *attract* aggression and predators.

And you know what?

No matter what you sell—or *how* you sell—if you are strong, you give off a much more attractive and persuasive "vibe" than if you are weak, out of shape, etc.

Think about it:

Who inspires more confidence?

1.   Someone who is 300 lbs overweight, weezing and can barely walk?

2.   Someone who looks weak, skinny and like a piece of chalk?

3.   Or someone who is fit, trim and strong—with a spring to their step and energy to their persona?

I am not judging anyone here.

But this is a simple sales and business fact. Get yourself in shape—and as *quickly* as possible—and you will find your sales go up *automatically*. This even works if you are not selling in *person*.

People can sense power and strength... as well as weakness and insecurity.

Crackerjack Selling Secret #34:
The #1 Easiest Way to Sell Ever Invented

This could very well be the *easiest* of all the Crackerjack Selling Secrets in this book.

In fact, there's a good chance you are *already* doing it without realizing it. And, if you are not already doing this, then I HIGHLY suggest starting ASAP.

Anyway, here's the secret:

**"Under Promise,
Over Deliver"**

I know, I know, it's cliche'.

But hokey as it sounds, this is THE secret to endless sales. And the beauty is, it works even if you aren't *thinking* about it. Reason why is because, when you under promise and over deliver you are almost always guaranteed to have a very *happy* customer. And a happy customer not only *refers* other people to you in abundance... but...

**Is Far More Likely
To Buy from You *Again!***

Even if your prices are higher.

Even if you don't necessary have the best product.

And even if you aren't the best "salesman" on the block.

When you over deliver and under promise, you are sort of "pre-selling" someone on something for the future. Do this right, and you will have already made the *next* sale of your product, idea, etc., *before* you even know what it's going to be.

Anyway, start thinking of ways to under promise and over deliver.

I think you will find selling easier (and more *profitable*) than ever before.

Crackerjack Selling Secret #35:
Put the Smack Down on the "Feel Good" Phonies

Remember earlier when I told you about Fred Herman on the old Johnny Carson show, who could sell without talking very much (Crackerjack Selling Secret #29)?

About how he asked questions and then shut up so people "sold themselves"?

Well, I once knew of a guy in MLM who did the same thing when selling his opportunity. He asked why they would want to be in a business like MLM and then let them talk. But there was another thing he did at the same time that was brilliant (and simple) persuasive selling in action.

Brilliant because of how *well* it works.

Simple because of how *easy* it is to do.

Anyway, after listening to his prospects give all the reasons for wanting to be in their own business, this MLM guy would then ask another important question:

"Those sound like important reasons, Mr. Prospect.
Are there any other reasons you'd want to be in business for yourself?"

At which point the prospect, after giving their "feel good", "logical" reasons for wanting to be in business for themselves, proceeded to give him the REAL reason—which was actually quite *emotional* and not logical at all.

Now, here's what's important about this:

Rarely will anyone tell you the *real* reason they want something on the first go. We all have a built-in "mechanism" where we say what we *think* the other person wants to hear, or that will make us look smarter, brighter and more sophisticated.

But the *real* reason is usually just the opposite.

It's *emotional* and may not even make *sense* to anyone else. And when you can get that emotional reason—the REAL reason—you will know what someone really wants so you can better serve them.

Which leads us to the Crackerjack Selling secret:

The best way to get to this real reason is to ask, when the other person is done talking:

"In addition to that,
is there anything else?"

Sounds pretty simple, doesn't it?

That's because it IS simple.

And it is one of the best, most reliable ways to get someone to lower their guards (Crackerjack Selling Secret #23) and tell you what they REALLY want (Crackerjack Selling Secret #2). Again, this is not meant to "trick" someone. If you truly *care* about someone's welfare and are trying to persuade them to buy something you know is good for them anyway... that they already *want* anyway... then this will help you do so.

Use it next time you get a chance and you will see exactly what I mean.

Crackerjack Selling Secret #36:
Threaten Their Families?

This Crackerjack Selling Secret, while 100% *ethical*, makes some people *squeamish*.

Whatever the case, here is a fact many salesmen and marketers who sell "prevention" type products have learned after spending thousands—even tens of thousands—of dollars in "trial and error": People will usually not spend a penny to prevent a nasty, painful or deadly problem when it comes to themselves, but...

They Will Take Out a Second Mortgage
To Save a *Loved One* from Pain!
It's weird, but true.

We have no problem with the idea of bad things happening to *us*—probably because we figure bad things only happen to "other" people.

But when it comes to our loved ones (who are "other" people) we get extremely *emotional*.

And so, if you are selling something that lends itself to protecting someone's family (like security or health-related products, for example) the best thing you can do is get them to visualize what could happen to their loved ones.

Now, don't be a *jerk* about it.

Treat them how you would want someone to treat you—with good taste and tact. But, as one famous life insurance salesmen once said:

"You have to make them see
the hearse pulled up
to the curb outside."

Kind of gruesome advice.

But extremely *accurate* nonetheless.

And so, if you sell a prevention type product or service, never forget people won't usually visualize bad things happening to them.

But they will (and *do*) visualize things happening to *others*.

Crackerjack Selling Secret #37:
Take the Pepsi Challenge

Remember those old TV commercials about the "Pepsi Challenge"?

Where the Pepsi people went around with two glasses of cola: One Pepsi, the other Coke, RC or some other cola? And then, the person who taste tested them would say which one they liked better—which (oh so conveniently) was Pepsi?

Well, guess what?

Dorky as they were... those commercials were a great Crackerjack Selling method called:

**"Invite Others
To Compare"**

In other words, instead of pretending your competition doesn't exist... acknowledge them and even *invite* your prospects to test them side by side.

This takes a lot of guts, and shows a lot of confidence in your product.

But if you do this, many times people will choose your product on the "spot"...

**Without Even Bothering
To Try Your Competition's Product!**

The fact you have THAT much confidence in your product is enough for them.

Remember, people are looking for someone they can trust and believe in. When you make bold, daring challenges like inviting them to compare your product to someone else's, you look like a *stud*. Many times, people (who are busy and don't want to mess around or waste time) will just assume you MUST be telling the truth. That you MUST have the best product. And that you MUST have a lot of faith in what you are selling.

Test it out the next time you are selling something with a lot of competition.

You may just see a nice "bump" in sales.

Crackerjack Selling Secret #38:
How to Sell with a Weak Pitch

Here is another easy way to ethically and consistently sell your products and services (especially if you are using direct marketing).

And it is pretty straight forward, too.

Yet, even so, it's amazing how few people focus on it. Listen, several years ago, a direct marketing sales genius named Ed Mayer came up with a nifty little formula for selling that goes like this:

1. Your list/customer is 40% of the sale.

2. Your offer is 40% of the sale.

3. Your sales pitch is 20% of the sale.

Interesting, isn't it?

Especially how little impact the actual "sales pitch" has compared to your offer and the desire your prospects have for the solution your product solves. And believe it or not, this is extremely *good* news. Because it means, even if your selling skills are *weak*, if you simply talk to someone who is *already* interested in what you sell (Crackerjack Selling Secret #2) and make them a strong OFFER...

You Almost
Can't Fail!

I mean, those two (non-sales technique) components are 80% of the battle.

While your actual words, or the mechanism for doing the actual selling (sales copy, speaking on stage, etc) is only 20% of the battle.

And many smart marketing pros have found that, if you attach a strong, "can't lose guarantee" to your offer, you make it...

A Total "No-Brainer" For People
To At Least Give You A Try.

One famous example of this is Domino's Pizza.

They went from being a tiny college-town joint on the brink of failure to a multi-million dollar powerhouse simply adding their famous: *"Hot fresh pizza in 30 minutes, or it's free"* offer. I once wrote an ad for the golf market (selling instructional videos) where the customer can try the DVD's free for 365 days. And if they aren't happy with the videos, they don't owe anything and can KEEP the videos for their trouble. They can't possibly lose.

See how that works?

You can do the same thing.

What's the most *outrageous* guarantee you can think of? The kind that makes people feel almost foolish for NOT buying?

Figure that out and you will often make two, three even four times as much money.

Crackerjack Selling Secret #39:
Bribe Your Way to the Bank

When you think of ethical selling—like the ones in this book—you probably don't think of this next Crackerjack Selling Secret:

Bribes.

After all, aren't bribes used by dirty politicians and their henchmen?

Yes they are, but I'm not talking about *those* kind of bribes.

I'm talking about...

***Ethical* Bribes.**

The late, great copywriting and marketing genius Gary Halbert made a *fortune* with these.

And they are perfect if you are selling a continuity-type product or service—something people buy over and over each month, like a newsletter, monthly maintenance service, magazine, health supplement, etc.

Basically, it goes like this:

You find something really valuable (usually an informational type product—such as a report, video, book, etc) and offer to give it to your customer *free*. But, you will ONLY give it to your customer free if they agree to a free "trial" of whatever it is you sell. So in other words, if you sell a newsletter, you could give your prospect a valuable report if they agree to "test drive" your newsletter for one month or a year or whatever. The gift is essentially a "bribe." But, as I mentioned, it is an *ethical* bribe. Usually (and I have never seen it done any other way) the customer can even KEEP the bribe...

**Even If They
Request a Refund!**

That's what makes the bribe ethical as well as gives your customers a strong incentive to give you a try.

Again, this can be applied to any kind of continuity type product or service, and it is one of the most tested and reliable ways of making the sale you can ever use.

Crackerjack Selling Secret #40:
The First Battle of the Sales "War"

This may seem overly simplified—but the whole key to selling is grabbing *attention*.

After all, if you don't first arrest someone's attention, you cannot sell them anything—whether in person, on the phone, in print or in any other medium. And one of the best ways to grab that attention is to simply...

**Startle Your
Prospect!**

Not necessarily *scare* him. But startle him. Wake him up, so to speak.

You can do so pretty easily if you begin with interesting facts about whatever problem your product or service solves. If you are communicating with the right kind of prospect then this is almost *guaranteed* to let you get your foot in the door. Think about it this way: If you had a burning, extremely *painful* urinary tract infection, and someone started telling you interesting facts and stories about how other people have overcome that problem, could you honestly NOT listen to every word?

All selling starts with grabbing attention (the old sales master Walter Dill Scott even coined this sales formula (AIDA)—*Attention, interest, desire, action*). And if you simply work in interesting facts about the painful problem or desire your prospect has, how can they ignore you?

They can't.

It's almost impossible if you show the right person the right solution. (Crackerjack Selling Secret #2.)

Crackerjack Selling Secret #41:
Sneak Your Way In

This Crackerjack Selling Secret is one of those "duh!" type secrets you may already be doing. But, if you are not, then I think you will find it extremely powerful (and effective.)

Anyway, here goes:

If you want to make your sales message (and this goes for ANY kind of selling) be *dramatically* more effective... have someone of the same age, gender, and other physical, professional and/or demographic as the customer...

Give the
Actual "Pitch"

In other words:

If you sell a product to senior citizens, have another senior citizen be the salesman or spokesman for it. Whether it's face-to-face selling, a written sales letter, video or whatever medium you use to sell your product. If you sell to a younger crowd, and you are over 25 or 30, then recruit a younger person to do your selling. If you are selling weight loss to middle-aged women then have another middle-aged woman do your selling. If you are selling to firemen, have another fireman give the pitch.

And so on, and so forth.

See how that works?

Most people are more likely to bond with and *trust...*

One of Their Own.

And that's why (in most cases) it's ideal to make your message come "from" someone in the exact same circumstances and/or demographic as your market. Whether it be physical looks, profession, religion or even *race* (Crackerjack Selling Secret #76).

It's one of the most powerful sales secrets you can use.

And can do more to advance the sale than most people realize.

Crackerjack Selling Secret #42:
Scare the *Hell* Out of Them

I am not a big fan of using "the sky is falling" scare tactics when selling.

But there's one time where using fear is not only highly effective... but also 100% ethical and honest. And that is simply using...

The Fear of Loss!

Fear of loss is actually more emotional and powerful than the desire for gain.

For whatever reason, we won't lift a finger to get something we don't already have. Not unless we REALLY want it, at least (Crackerjack Selling Secrets #2). But we will crawl through jagged pieces of broken *glass* to prevent someone from taking something we *already* possess. This is why, for example, direct marketers sometimes send customers a letter saying they won a prize and then give a time frame to pick it up.

Even if they didn't want the prize originally, many will be motivated to pick up that prize because it's "theirs." It's got *their* name on it!

And so it just makes sense to go get it—

Even if They Didn't
Originally *Want* It.

This is most easily applied to retail type businesses, but goes for almost anything you sell. Just ask: How can you project ownership of something to your customers? So, they feel like your product is *already* theirs?

Figure that out and selling will get way easier for you.

Crackerjack Selling Secret #43:
A Secret Way to "Out Fox" Sales Resistance

One of the best business books I own is *How to Out Fox the Foxes* by Larry Williams.

And while the book is primarily about how to "stick it" to greedy lawyers, bureaucrats, and other scum thinking up ways to steal from hard-working entrepreneurs, it also contains an extremely powerful sales tip. You can find it on page 78. And it basically says:

**"People move towards pleasure
and away from pain"**

How does this help with your selling?

It goes back to creating vision (<u>Crackerjack Selling Secret #4</u>). If you show people how your product or service will help them avoid nasty problems and pain... and instead give them pleasure, happiness and peace of mind... the sale is as good as made in most cases. In the book, Mr. Williams talks about using this strategy to persuade people not to want to sue you by making them realize how costly and draining the process is.

You can use this same concept in selling, too.

Paint that picture of the pain they will avoid... and the pleasure they will gain... from buying from you. Do it honestly, ethically, and in good taste, of course. But if there's a deep, dark pain your product or service can help people avoid make sure you describe it in full detail.

I don't care if you're selling "belly to belly", in print, on TV or anywhere else.

Show how what you got will move them towards pleasure and away from pain... and you will be doing them a true service.

Crackerjack Selling Secret #44:
How to Get Products to Sell Themselves

Interesting story:

Several years ago, I used to slug it out day after day in MLM. The company I was in (long since dissolved) sold health and nutrition supplements. And I always found it a really tough sell. No matter how much I tried... no matter how well I followed the phone scripts and sales trainers... no matter how much passion and enthusiasm I had (even if I had to *fake* it)... the fish just weren't "biting" for me.

It used to dumbfound and frustrate me to no ends.

And I could never figure out what the "bottleneck" in my business was. Why could I NOT consistently sell a product so potent it should have sold itself? Fast forward several years later, and I now understand why. Instead of selling "prevention" (as we were told to do)...

I Should Have Been
Selling *Cures*.

For example, instead of trying to "convince" people how my herbal supplement would prevent prostate problems... I should have been finding people who *already* had prostate problems and focused on them.

Common sense?

Well, yes and no.

Unfortunately, all the sales training I got seemed to revolve around gimmicks, enthusiasm and persistence. But if we just use a few simple principles, such as finding out what people *already* want (Crackerjack Selling Secret #2)... instead of trying to prevent things that people don't ever see happening to them (Crackerjack Selling Secret #36)... then selling gets really easy. In fact, people in pain are often *actively* searching for something to help them. And it is not an imposition to show them what you have.

Anyway, here's the point:

Whatever your product or service, if you concentrate on those who need a cure, instead of those you think need a prevention, you will instantly sell more with less hassle.

In fact, they will often "sell themselves" on your product.

Crackerjack Selling Secret #45:
Persuasion Time Machine

Many years ago (before she "caught on"), I used to *sell* a girl I was with on running errands for me I was fully capable of running myself. (Yeah, it was pretty cool...)

And the way I used to persuade her is...

Worth Solid Gold
If You Have
Something to Sell.

You see, what would happen is, she would already be going somewhere—the store, gas station, mall, etc.

And what I'd do right before she left is say, *"Hey, since you're already going, can you stop by (wherever I wanted her to go) and pick me up (whatever it is I wanted her to pick up)?"* Of course, since she was already out, she would tell me no problem and do it.

Now, here's what's instructive:

Had I asked her to run these errands (usually frivolous errands for dorky things) at any other TIME—such as if she was relaxing or doing something—she would have denied me.

Probably even *laughed* at them.

Because, as we saw in Crackerjack Selling Secret #16...

Timing Is
***Everything* in Sales.**

Fact is, even if you follow the advice from earlier (Crackerjack Selling Secret #2) of finding out what people already want, they may not be *ready* to buy it now. And if you can arrange the timing of the sale to happen at the *ideal* time, then your chances of making the sale go up dramatically. An example of this would be asking for a second sale after they just bought from you, and already have their checkbook out. ("want fries with that?") Or asking for a customer testimonial or referral right after someone has said something nice about you. Or asking the boss for a raise after you do something he or she praises you to the moon for.

It's all about timing.

Get your timing right and you can't help but sell more.

Crackerjack Selling Secret #46:
Learn A "Foreign" Language

One of my favorite copywriting teachers is a guy named David Garfinkel.

Not only is he one of my favorites, but he even has the reputation of being "The World's Greatest Copywriting Coach." And he got that reputation for probably several *reasons*. One of which is his ability to get "inside" the heads of those he wants to sell to. I heard an interview he did once where he talked about this in detail. And his advice made things a LOT easier for me when selling—both in print and in person.

Here is what he said (paraphrased):

When researching his market and customers, just as important as knowing what the *problem* is they want to solve, is the *words* they use to *describe* the problem.

This is HUGE.

A lot of businesses are "product centered" instead of "customer centered."

And the way *you* may describe their problem could be WAY different than how your *customer* describes it. Which means, if you can figure out the exact language, words and phrases your customers use to describe the problem your product or service solves (i.e. "talk the talk")...

**Your Chances
Of Making the Sale
Rise Dramatically!**

So, make sure you study not only the problem your customers needs solving... but the *way* they *describe* that problem. This helps make you "one of them" (Crackerjack Selling Secret #41)—someone they can TRUST. Someone who has their best interests at heart (Crackerjack Selling Secret #1). And someone who is *easier* to spend money with than everyone else.

Crackerjack Selling Secret #47:
The Power of One

I once heard an incredibly valuable lesson from top marketing coach Dan Kennedy. It went like this:

"One is the most
dangerous number
in business."

Why is this so important?

Because if you rely on one big customer, one good vendor, one service provider, one client or one of *anything* else—you are setting yourself up for some major problems when "one" of those people alters their policies, changes their businesses or simply quits altogether.

But here's the thing: While one may be the most *dangerous* number in business, it is...

The Most *Important*
Number in Sales!

Why?

Because, as many seasoned salesmen, marketers and copywriters have discovered... trying to sell more than one thing at a time is sales *suicide*. Reason why is because people don't want a lot of choices or to *think* at all when buying.

I'm not saying they don't have the ability to think.

But most people don't want to *have* to.

We're all busy with a million things going on in our lives. We want things *easy*, *pleasant* and *fast*. And there is no better way to take this "burden" off your customer's shoulders than by selling only one product, service, idea, etc at a time.

Keep your sales presentation to one product and one product only. Every time you introduce another "moving part" into the equation, you increase the chances you will kill the sale.

Crackerjack Selling Secret #48:
Tap into Your Childhood Angst

It's amazing what we'll do to get the approval of authority figures when we're kids. In many cases that's a child's one biggest goal—get the approval of people. This is why kids sometimes do stupid things that make no sense and enter careers or jobs they hate.

However, it's not just kids and young adults who do this.

"Grown Ups"
Are the Same Way.

We *crave* approval.

Which is why, if you can show people how buying your product or service will secure the *approval* of others, you will often *dramatically* increase your sales. This is why so many of the best advertisements, for example, spend time explaining how herbal supplement X is approved by doctors in 54 different countries.

Approval is everything to a lot of people—even those who like to play "rebel."

Because, after all, what is the rebel in us really trying to do other than get the approval of other rebels and non-conformists?

Anyway, here's the point:

If you want to sell more, show how your product helps prospects get the *approval* of others. This is one of the reasons getting to know your market and prospects at a deeper level (Crackerjack Selling Secret #46) can make all the difference.

People will go to insane lengths to gain the approval of others.

Show them how your product will get it for them, and you'll increase your sales big time.

Crackerjack Selling Secret #49:
Give Them a "Treat"

Want a quick and easy way to persuade someone to buy from you or, at the very *least*, send you abundant referrals? Then simply do what they used to do in the old west to get people to turn in blood-thirsty murderers and horse thieves:

Offer A Reward!

In fact, I believe you should reward anyone who helps you—whether they are buying, referring or giving you good word-of-mouth promotion—as *often* as possible.

It all comes down to this simple "rule" of human nature:

When you reward people for doing something... they will do whatever "thing" they did to get rewarded again and again and again.

For example:

If someone refers a big client to you, and you send them a big, fat box of steaks (or some other gift they will love), then guess what will happen?

There's A Good Chance
They Will Refer
Even *More* Clients
To You Again!

You can apply this to customers, vendors, and anyone else you can think of.

We're all the same at heart. We're all basically like the little dog who, after you reward him with a treat for sitting or heeling, will be more likely to sit or heel when asked next time. It's just the way we are (especially those of us in *sales*).

And rewarding those who help you sell is almost guaranteed to inspire the same behavior next time.

Crackerjack Selling Secret #50:
The Secret of Scientific Telepathy

Did you know you have *telepathic* powers? Did you know you can, for all practical purposes, read the minds of your customers? And did you further know that, if you simply use this "power" (you were *born* with), you can make selling a near no-brainer?

I know it sounds strange, but it's absolutely true.

Whatever your business... whatever you sell... and however you sell it (whether in face to face, advertising, tele-marketing, etc.)... you can get a "snapshot" of what your customer desires (even if secretly) simply by...

Looking at Your
Junk Mail!

Or by reading the ads in your newspaper and magazines.

Or by listening to the sales pitches on the radio.

Or by paying attention to everywhere else where you see direct response advertising (i.e. advertising that asks for you to "respond" either by phone, internet, mail, fax, etc.).

Most people don't realize this but, in direct response advertising, all the hard work of what appeals and emotional "hot buttons" your customers have...

Has Already Been Done
For **You!**

Often *millions* of dollars in scientific testing has been conducted to create these ads on the EXACT emotions, fears, desires and "hot buttons" your customers have right now.

In many cases, every word, phrase and idea has been carefully tested against other words, phrases and ideas to see which one pulls the most sales. And that's why, if you simply observe what someone is *already* buying (that is related to what you sell), and then see how others are successfully selling that same product or service, you can "hijack" those sales arguments and use them in YOUR selling.

In other words, if you see a certain appeal working in successful ads (and you can tell an ad is successful by if it is being repeatedly run over and over and over), use it in YOUR sales presentations and see what happens. And it doesn't matter how you're selling either. It can be over the phone, in person, on the Internet or through the mail. These appeals have been tested over and over and are...

Hitting A "Nerve"

I am not saying to 100% rely on this information (especially if you are selling person-to-person or on the phone, where you can and should ask questions and probe).

But this neat little "shortcut" really can save you a bundle of time and energy.

Crackerjack Selling Secret #51:
How even Bad Salesmen Can Make out Like Bandits

Have you ever noticed how many times the sales person who is the LEAST "polished"... the LEAST "well-spoken"... or the LEAST competent with the keyboard... can out-sell everyone around them?

Well, one reason they get away with that is because, what they lack in technique...

They More Than
Make Up for In Passion!

Passion can move *mountains*.

It can get a complete "nobody" elected to public office. It can start entire movements that take a life of their own. And it can help you...

Sell Like You've Been
At It for Decades!

Even if you are wet behind the ears and don't really know what you're doing.

And it works because people are *attracted* to passion. Passion is one of those things everyone wants to have more of in their life—personal, professional and everything in between. But for some reason, passion is also the one thing people are most *unwilling* to use in sales.

Example?

Few years ago, I hired a new accountant who is like this. He's just really "in" to numbers—and figuring out tax strategies, etc. He's so into it you can't help but get into it, too. And it gives you 100% confidence in his services where you are almost *happy* to pay him. Because that enthusiasm, if it's real, is really contagious no matter what you're selling.

Get *passionate* about what you sell, too.

Don't hold back or let anyone dampen that fire. Passion is a rare asset—like gold or silver—in this world.

Use it and watch your sales grow.

Crackerjack Selling Secret #52:
"Doctor" Your Evidence

I've talked a lot about my MLM days already. And as much as I hated doing MLM, it gave me one of the best sales educations I could ask for.

Take, for example, when I was just starting out as a distributor for an MLM company selling health and wellness products.

I was on fire!

I went to all the symposiums, rallies and events. I read everything the product creators wrote and memorized the studies and benefits of the products. I even traveled hundreds of miles just to see hear people *speak*. Yet, when I got home and told people about how our supplement was better than any prescription drugs people were taking... or why their doctors were flat out wrong about how to deal with certain problems... or what people needed to do to get better health...

**I Was Met with
Blank Stares!**

Often, I was flat out ignored (and even *scoffed* at).

Why?

Because I was a "layman" trying to contradict an already *established* belief backed up by professional doctors. When I figured this out, it was a true "duh!" moment.

This happens in direct marketing all the time.

You can have the most fascinating product in the world. But unless it's "knighted" by a doctor, lawyer, military general, or whatever authority people trust in your particular niche...

**Nobody Will
Believe You!**

Which is why, if you want to increase your sales, back up your claims with *authority*.

For example, if you sell homeopathic remedies, get a doctor's endorsement. If you sell a new kind of tractor, get the endorsement of a major farm organization. If you sell a book on how to lose weight by eating more fatty foods, get the "blessing" of a well-respected fitness trainer.

And so on and so forth.

As the great marketer Gary Bencivenga says:

"Nobody Buys

86

Without Belief"

This is especially true when it comes to going against the "dogma" of your market.

Crackerjack Selling Secret #53:
The Cure Is in the Symptom

As we saw in <u>Crackerjack Selling Secret #41</u>, some of the best sales pitches spend a lot of time letting you know you are "one of them."

People love to listen to (and *buy* from) people just like them, and who have been where they are now.

And here's one simple way to do it: Tell a story **(**<u>Crackerjack Selling Secret #3</u>**)** where you are the main "character"... and how you overcame the *exact* same challenges as those you are selling to.

Sound almost too easy?

Maybe so. But this strategy is so reliable and effective...

**It Works Almost
Every Time It's Used!**

What makes it work so well?

For one thing, it makes people *bond* with you in a way no credentials, degrees or any other credibility elements can. This is why so many sales pitches and presentations start with someone's *personal* story. Where they talk about how they started out dead broke with barely enough money to eat or make rent. Or how they were overweight their entire lives, getting laughed at and picked on by their peers. Or how they were in so much debt they almost considered *suicide*.

And so on.

Heck, even old comic book ads did this in the form of comic strips. The old Charles Atlas ads did this all day long—where the skinny kid on the beach gets sand kicked in his face in front of his girl and seeks revenge. I remember my boss at my first sales job (selling discounted CBS TV advertising) saying this is how he built his business. He was a Cuban immigrant who came to the U.S., noticed small business owners struggling to pay for TV ads, and discovered a way to make it cheap for them to advertise on CBS. That simple story opened up customers' minds (and *wallets*) in a way no fancy presentation of facts and figures ever could.

Anyway, here's the point:

By telling a story showing you had the *exact* same problems and "symptoms" as those you are selling to...

**You Instantly
Bond with Them.**

And as a result, you become much more "trustworthy."

You are one of THEM.

Which is why, if you want to sell faster, easier and more effectively... show your customers you were once in their *shoes*.

And that you know exactly how it feels to be in their position.

Crackerjack Selling Secret #54:
Turning Lemons into Ice Cream

One important (and little talked about) business secret—that can help anyone sell more products and services—is the "art" of turning angry customers into happy customers.

No matter who you are, how well you treat people, and how *infrequently* you screw up, eventually you will—probably through no fault of your own—have a horde of angry customers at your door step—torches and pitch forks in hand demanding your head. When that happens, your ability to sell those angry customers on relaxing and putting their pitchforks down will be worth more money to you than all the slick sales one-liners and "choke holds" combined.

Why?

Because if you can make things right, not only will those customers *forgive* you... but...

They'll Become
The *Best* Customers
You Ever Have!

The kind that trust you

That *believe* in you.

And that will not want to do business with anyone else *but* you.

Only question is, how do you "flip" angry customers into happy buyers like this? Probably the best example of doing this is from direct marketing genius Dan Kennedy when he once said:

"It's hard to be mad at someone
who gives you ice cream."

He was talking about how some airline had dropped the ball on its passengers and, to make up for it, they gave everyone free ice cream. At that moment, everyone went from extremely *angry*... to extremely *happy*.

And in about 5 seconds all was forgiven.

This has worked in other circumstances, too. For example, a person who saved her job after making a terrible mistake by buying everyone at the office a pizza and donuts the next day.

The point?

It's hard to be angry or mad at someone who does nice things for you. (Especially if food is involved.) I hate to say this (but it's true) it's such a powerful psychological phenomenon it lets even *abusive* people—including the ones who do truly evil things to other people—get away with their abuse for years.

Of course, this then begs the question:

How can you utilize this principal in your business?

Answer: If you make a mistake—no matter what it is—immediately send out a letter apologizing profusely. And in addition to apologizing... give the offended parties a gigantic deal so unbelievably generous...

**They Can't *Help* but Like
And Buy from You!**

For example:

Let's say you sell a line of information products on making money, and you did something to royally tick off your list. If you want to get back on their "good side" simply tell them they can pick any one of your products for 90% off and get another one free (or something to that effect).

In other words, offer them something they can't refuse and will feel good about getting.

Your customers win because they are getting a tremendous deal. You win because you keep the customer and (if you do it right) pocket a little profit at the same time. Frankly, I have heard of marketing campaigns "gone bad" that actually came out way ahead due to wise usage of this principal.

Anyway, keep this tip handy for future reference.

It'll not only save you a lot of money—but it can possibly even *make* you money (imagine <u>making</u> money from your *mistakes*), too.

Crackerjack Selling Secret #55:
How to Automatically Attract More Sales

I will admit, this Crackerjack Selling secret will seem almost impossible, at first.

But trust me, it's not. As outrageous as it seems on the surface, it's actually much *easier* to pull off than most people think.

Anyway, here's what it's about:

You've no doubt noticed how many companies recruit celebrities to "star" in their ads, corporate events and as spokespeople. Now, some people may think they do this because of these particular stars' sales ability. But it simply ain't so. You see, most of these celebrities probably don't know *anything* about selling. BUT... what they DO have...

Is Star Power!

And this is immensely *powerful* if you can harness it for your business.

How so?

Because when you recruit a celebrity—whether a TV star, sports celebrity or even a local politician (anyone who is both respected and in the "spotlight")—you *automatically* attract more attention and money. This goes back to publicity. (Crackerjack Selling Secret #15.) Like it or not, experts and authorities don't get the attention and money anymore.

The *celebrities* do.

Which is why, if you can recruit a celebrity for your business, you will give yourself a...

**Huge Advantage
Over Your Competition!**

And here's the best part:

It's not hard to get celebrities to do this for you. Some will do it for money. Others will do it if you donate money to their favorite cause. Others can be negotiated with for other kinds of payment. And don't think it has to be a "big name" movie or TV star. A celebrity is anyone in the spotlight—local or national. Your mayor is a celebrity. As is your local high school sports hero. Or a local news anchor, police chief, radio DJ, etc. Really, anyone in the spotlight who is not mired in scandal is a celebrity you can use. And if you want to deal with bigger names—there's a book called *The Black Book of Celebrities* on Amazon.com.

Just grab that book and start contacting them.

You might be surprised how easy it is to recruit TV and movie stars to help you sell.

Crackerjack Selling Secret #56:
Spider-man's Persuasion Secret

I don't know about you... but I *loved* collecting comic books as a kid.

I enjoyed them so much, I even wanted to *be* a comic book writer or artist, prompting me to spend a lot of time reading interviews with comic book creators. And although I didn't realize it at the time, reading these interviews taught me one of the most powerful sales secrets on the planet.

Here's what I mean:

Whenever these comic book pros were asked why they got into the business or what made them start reading comics, many of them would say that yes, they loved the action and adventure and artwork, etc. But even more than that… they wanted to see what was going on in Spider-Man's love life. Or what Batman did when he wasn't kicking butt on the streets at night. Or if Clark Kent was ever gonna finally "get it on" with Lois Lane.

Anyway, here's my point:

It became obvious people don't just buy comic books for the usual reasons of action, adventure, great stories and riveting art. They're also buying...

A Personality!

They're buying someone they can *identify* with each month—with the same hopes, dreams, problems, fears and insecurities as everyone else. In fact, Stan Lee (the co-creator of Spider-Man) said his biggest challenge writing Spider-Man was not coming up with dialogue or new villains for him to fight. No, his biggest challenge was actually creating more *problems* to throw at Spider-Man when he wasn't in his spidey suit and was just Peter Parker. He wanted to make sure people identified with Spider-Man not just as a "super hero"… but also as a *regular* person, too.

The result?

Spider-Man is a world-famous icon who's been worth billions of dollars to Marvel Comics. Kids and adults both flock to Spider-Man movies and talk about him with their friends. And money is attracted to Spidey in huge quantities.

That's the Power of
Displaying Personality!

And guess what?

You can easily harness this "power" (no pun intended) yourself for selling. The key is to just let your hair down and be yourself. Don't try to be the stiff, perfectly "polished" speaker, presenter or (if you're using advertising) *writer*.

Use your own peculiar figures of speech, attitude and colloquialisms.

In a lot of ways, using your personality makes selling easier anyway. You don't get hung up on rules, techniques and "tactics." You may even butcher a few major sales "rules" every now and then.

But who cares?

At least you're being "real" so people will feel like you're talking *to* them, not *at* them. And the difference in results can be like night and day.

Crackerjack Selling Secret #57:
How to use Controversy to Attract Customers

The following may be one of the most *unusual* sales tips you will ever hear. It may even seem crazy. But if you use it, you may very well see a huge difference in your results. And I'll explain it with a real-life example. (By the way, this example pertains to written selling—copywriting—but it can just as easily apply to ANY kind of selling.)

Here's the story:

A while back, I wrote an ad for a high-selling self-defense DVD series that was somewhat "controversial." One person I showed it to got mad when reading it, and declared there is no way *anyone* would buy from it.

Reason why he said that is because it offended his political views and...

Made Him Furious!

As soon as I heard his anger, I was confident it would be a *hit*.

Why?

Because the ad was not written to ALL self-defense enthusiasts. Instead, it was specifically written to a segment of the market that has strong right-wing views when it comes to crime, terrorism and illegal immigration.

Our market research (Crackerjack Selling Secret #5) clearly showed the market we were selling to listened to a lot of talk radio each day while driving to and from their high paying jobs. These were conservative white males, who listen to shows like Michael Savage, Rush Limbaugh and other right-wing talk.

And so, when writing the ad, I wrote to them—and them, *only*.

In some cases, the copy sounded more like a transcript of the Michael Savage or Rush Limbaugh show than an "ad." It addressed that specific market's fears, angers and opinions about issues like illegal immigration, socialists in Congress, and the rise of legal "loopholes" that often let criminals, rapists and even cold-blooded killers off the hook for their crimes.

And my friend, who is NOT part of this market, was *appalled*.

It insulted his beliefs and caused him to want to argue with some of the conclusions and opinions in the piece.

Which I took as a *good* sign.

Because as strange as it sounds, meantime, good sales pitches will...

Repel **as Many People**
As They *Attract*!

There should be no "luke warm" reactions to a sales letter.

Either people respond to it, or they are *repelled* by it.

And it's the same with any kind of persuasive selling—whether a sales "letter" or not. Frankly, you can often pre-judge the power of your message simply by how many people are repulsed by it. And again, even though the example is about copywriting—it can apply to any sales medium. When selling, talk ONLY to your prospects—THEIR problems, concerns and fears—and forget about what everyone else thinks. If you aren't deliberately offending certain people, then there's a good chance you are not going to get the response you are looking for.

Crackerjack Selling Secret #58:
Give 'Em Bragging Rights

Brag, brag, brag.

Seems that's all a lot of people do when they are selling something. All they want to do is brag about everything—their product, their company, themselves.

However, the problem is, they are bragging about the *wrong* thing.

And they are making a huge mistake. Because the person they should REALLY be bragging about...

Is Their *Customers*.

Here's what I mean:

One of the strongest urges most people have (even if they are too polite to admit it) is they want to be able to brag about something—*anything*—to their friends, family and in-laws. Call it a competitive streak or whatever you want. But there it is. And that's why, when selling somebody something, one thing that will help you close the sale is to show them how buying what you have will *elevate* them in the eyes of their family, friends, peers, co-workers, etc.

This may seem odd, but people desperately want to have...

"Bragging Rights"

They want to be able to brag about the cool "thing" they just bought, or the great deal they finagled from the salesman, or anything that lets them have their moment in the spotlight.

Hey, we're ALL like this, too.

So, this is not something to look down at people about. It's just the way people think. And if you can "tap" into this emotion, then your chances of persuading someone to buy or do what you want, is greatly magnified.

Crackerjack Selling Secret #59:
Get Others to Do Your Dirty Work

Back in the "old days" of the wild west, whenever someone committed a serious crime (murder, horse stealing, etc), the sheriff would often post a sign saying the criminal was wanted...

Dead or Alive!

And, to give people an "incentive" to jump on horseback and travel through oven-like deserts, freezing cold nights and the worst kind of weather and conditions you can imagine (often with little food or water), they would offer a reward. Usually a fat reward that would be enough to help someone struggling financially to pay off some nagging debt or whatever.

And you can do the same thing when selling today.

Here's what I mean:

Sometimes the best "sales people" are not the sales and marketing guys.

No...

It's Your Customers!

Especially *satisfied* customers.

And if you simply give your satisfied customers a reward for referring other people to you—where 9 out of 10 times the people they refer are in a state of being "pre-sold", and ready (even *eager*) to buy—near-*magical* things start to happen. Reason why is because nothing is more persuasive than the real-life testimony of another person they know, like and trust. Nobody trusts salesmen or "pitches." But we do trust what our friends and family think. And if you simply give your customers some kind of *reward*—which can be literally anything—they will be much more likely to refer others to you in abundance.

Plus, if you remember Crackerjack Selling Secret #49, not only will they be likely to refer to you... but KEEP referring to you.

Because being rewarded will make them far more likely to...

Keep Sending You
Paying Customers in the Future!

Anyway, here's the point:

Your happy customers are your best valuable *asset*.

Give an incentive or reward for telling others about you and watch your sales explode.

Crackerjack Selling Secret #60:
Understatement Underdogs

One of the most solid persuasive selling lessons ever told is found in an old 1970's ad as told by advertising "giant" Gary Bencivenga.

Many years ago, an ad was run with the headline:

"Why the Price Of Silver
May Rise Steeply"

When Gary Bencivenga came on board to help with that company's advertising, the word "may" bothered him. It didn't sound as confident as, say, "Why the Price Of Silver **'Will'** Rise Steeply." So, the agency Gary was working for decided to test using "Will" instead of "May."

The result?

Believe it or not, the split test showed FAR more response (something like 200% more sales) for the ad using "May" in the headline, than the ad with "Will"—even though it sounds "weaker", and even though most people would not even think to use "may" at all.

Moral of the story?

People are not dumb. They are not stupid. And they are not without...

Strong "BS meters"

Any *scent* of hype can often ruin a sale.

Which is why using *understatements*—including words like "almost", "some", "may", "might", etc.—before making a promise or claim can make your pitch FAR more *credible* and *believable*. Both of which build trust. And, as we learned in Crackerjack Selling Secret #1, people are far more likely to buy from people they trust.

So instead of using hype, you are better off under-selling and *understating*, instead.

That doesn't mean you should not use your strongest benefits and promises. But "temper" them with understatements.

It will make everything you say more believable and (thus) more *persuasive*.

Crackerjack Selling Secret #61:
Three Letters That Move Mountains

Did you know you can ethically sell more products with less effort by using just three letters in the alphabet?

But before showing you these 3 letters, let's talk about the two WORST letters (for selling) in the alphabet:

The first one is "M-E." ("I" is a no-no, too.)

You ever see someone trying to sell and all they can do is talk about themselves? All they do is brag about how superior their product or service is? How it's the best thing in the world? And why the prospect or customer **NEEDS TO HAVE IT!!!**

Well, that's not only incredibly ineffective... but it's also...

Incredibly *Stupid* Too!

And this goes for any kind of sales—in person, in print, online, whatever.

So instead of using "Me" (and "I") all the time, use these 3 letters instead: Y-O-U.

I've talked about Eugene Schwartz (the great copywriter) several times in this book. And one of the best sales lessons he ever taught (in a speech he gave) was:

"If an ad doesn't have the word 'you' in it 100 times,
I really don't like it very much."

In other words... the word "you" should be in your ad as much as possible.

Not only to help the customer feel like you're talking directly to him or her... but also to

make the "bonding" process between you and the reader that much more *intense*.

And again, this applies to ANY kind of persuasion—not just copywriting.

Saying things like...

"Mr. Jones, tell me about what YOU are doing?" Or, "Mrs. Smith, why exactly might YOU want a new widget?" Or, "Here is what YOU do to use this widget. Apply it to YOUR yard, and then go back into your YOUR home for a few hours. When YOU come back, YOU will see..."

... can go a LONG way towards helping you increase your sales.

Make your sales pitches more "you-ful" and you can't go wrong.

Crackerjack Selling Secret #62:
Nuke the Lukewarm

Ever read the Bible?

Specifically, the Book of Revelation? Believe it or not, there's a powerful selling secret in Revelation 3:16 when God is talking to a church He was displeased with:

"So then because thou art lukewarm, and neither cold nor hot, I will spew thee out of My mouth."

How is this a sales lesson?

Because God's attitude towards the "lukewarm" can be directly applied to *selling*, too. In fact, dealing with a lukewarm prospect can drive you *insane*.

It's far better to get a solid "yes" or "no"—and as *quickly* as possible.

That's why I like asking questions such as, "Why don't you think about it for 5 minutes and then let me know if you want it or not." Or, "It sounds like you've been thinking about this a while. There are far more important things to think about than this, why don't you just tell me no and let me go on my way?" Or, "Listen, if this isn't for you, if it's not what you're looking for, just tell me no, okay?"

And so on.

This is important if you want to keep your sanity and not waste time. Messing with lukewarm prospects...

Will Only
Frustrate You!

Which is why, if you want to be better at selling, spend your time qualifying and "sifting" so the people you talk to are either hot or cold.

If someone is *hot*, great!

If they're *cold*, that's good too—because you can move on and not waste any more time with them.

But if you are dealing with someone who is *lukewarm* then it's best to get them to make a decision as fast as possible. Ask them for a yes or no—with "maybe" not being an option. If they say yes, they obviously go into the hot camp and you can go for the sale. If they say no, they obviously go into the cold camp and you can move on. If they say "maybe"...

Then You *Move*
Them into No.

Just tell them it's not for them and move on.

They will either let you go or, due to the "takeaway effect" (Crackerjack Selling Secret #14), they could go into the "hot" camp.

Whatever the case, you don't want someone staying lukewarm.

Crackerjack Selling Secret #63:
Abraham Lincoln's long-lost Persuasion secret

Like him or not, Abraham Lincoln was one of the great "persuaders" in history.

Lincoln even used many of the secrets in this book to become president. And one of the best persuasion "secrets" he used were both simple and *brilliantly* effective: Before stating his position on a matter, he would demonstrate a sympathetic and *genuine* understanding of the other person's position (no matter how much he disagreed with it) *first*.

This may seem almost too simple.

But it taps into multiple different Crackerjack Selling strategies. Like genuinely caring (Crackerjack Selling Secret #1) about the other person. Shutting up (Crackerjack Selling Secret #29). And asking questions (Crackerjack Selling Secret #3).

Very powerful stuff.

And by not attacking, belittling or "twisting" the other person's position or belief (which is what many of us do naturally if we don't "catch" ourselves), he would give himself an enormous advantage. Especially since now the other person would be...

Much More Likely to Hear
And Understand HIS Side.

This easy mindset "shift" can do wonders for you, too.

And in many ways, it's essential.

Because if you don't hear your prospects out before "pitching" them anything, how can you know what they really *want* (Crackerjack Selling Secret #2)? How can you know what they really *need* from you that can improve their lives? How can you truly know how to *serve* them? (And make them so happy with your service they can't help but tell their friends about you and keep coming back for more?)

The beauty of this is, it's as easy and ethical as the day is long.

Just give your customers (and this is especially true of skeptical and even *angry* customers—Crackerjack Selling Secret #85) a good listening to.

Hear them out.

At that point, you've "earned" the right to make YOUR case for buying your product.

Crackerjack Selling Secret #64:
How Smart Door-to-Door Salesmen did it

Back in the era of door-to-door salesmen, it was pretty rough sailing for salesmen.

I have heard all kinds of door-to-door sales "war stories"—where they had to stick their foot in the door to get an audience with someone, then persuade the prospect to let him come in and demonstrate whatever it was he was selling.

But you know what?

It wasn't like that for everyone. In fact, a few (really smart) salesmen figured out a different way of selling. A way practically *devoid* of frustration and rejection.

What did they do? The answer is simple. Instead of knocking and selling, they would...

**Offer a Free
Consultation!**

And it worked like *gangbusters*.

Why?

Because, remember when we talked about demonstration (Crackerjack Selling Secret #11)? How it is one of the single best ways to persuade someone your product does what you say? Well, there is simply no easier way to do that—with a *willing* audience, no less—than by giving a free consultation on whatever it is you sell.

If you think about it, a free consultation is nothing more than a big demonstration.

And it is a MUCH easier commitment to make than making an outright pitch and asking someone to buy on the spot. Now, obviously, it's much more common for service providers to do this than product sellers. But even if you have a product, you can still make it work.

Simply offer a free consultation not on your product, but the PROBLEM it solves.

Like a nutritionist, for example, giving a free consult on why someone is constipated (and then offering his best supplement as the solution later on).

See how that works?

This way you get to use multiple Crackerjack Selling Secrets at once: Demonstration, asking questions, positioning, and even *authority*.

Anyway, think long and hard about what you can offer as a free consultation.

I can virtually guarantee you will see much better results.

Crackerjack Selling Secret #65:
Ask Squirmy Questions

This Crackerjack Selling Secret is related to #62 about *lukewarm* prospects.

As you'll remember, it's vital to get prospects off the "fence"—either as buyers or not.

With no dilly-dally or "hemming and hawing."

That way you can focus your time and efforts on the "foxes" and not the "dogs." But, sometimes getting them off that fence can be a bit tricky. Sometimes people will *insist* on being lukewarm (it feels "safe" for many people) and come up with very creative ways to...

STAY Lukewarm.

So in those cases, what do you do?

How do you get them from lukewarm to hot (or cold)?

One of the best ways I've seen comes from genius sales trainer "Shameless" Shamus Brown. And what he does is...

Ask *Squirmy* Questions!

Such as questions about their finances.

About their *personal* lives.

About their pain and misery.

And about anything else *relevant* that will either turn them off or on... so you can get to the heart of what they really want.

For example:

You can ask them how it will feel if they don't solve whatever problem they have (or how *wonderful* it will feel once they DO solve it.) You could also ask them what it would be worth to their lives to solve the problem that your product solves. You could even question them about what *lengths* they are willing to go to avoid the pain they have or how that pain is going to affect their personal, professional and family life (all depending on the situation, of course.)

Will some people get angry or offended?

Yes!

And that's what you *want*—a reaction and decision that is either...

Hot or Cold!

As we already saw, cold is just as good because now you can move on. So don't be afraid to ask the tough questions. Sometimes it's necessary for you to help someone decide whether they should buy or not.

And let's face it:

If what you have is truly valuable, and can really HELP them, then you are doing people a DISSERVICE by not forcing them make a decision one way or the other.

Crackerjack Selling Secret #66:
Opposite Adams

One of my all-time favorite books (actually, it's more of a pamphlet) is an old story from 1916 called *Obvious Adams*. This is a short story about an advertising man who was not the best or most skilled copywriter… but whose ads were ultra-successful simply because he knew how to spot the "obvious" solutions to problems.

It's an absolutely fascinating read.

And it teaches a special kind of "mindset" you won't find in other sales books.

However, while reading it, I started thinking about another "character" just as important as old "Obvious."

Someone I like to call...

"Opposite Adams"

Earl Nightingale, one of the great success teachers of the past 100 years, said if you want to succeed, all you have to do is look around at what everyone else is doing... and do the exact *opposite*.

I have found this to be *especially* true in selling.

Which is why I believe one of the best ways to sell is to look around at how your competition is selling and test doing the exact *opposite*. This lets you stick out from the crowd, get immediately noticed and, if you do it right...

Be Far More *Trusted.*

It also gives you an air of "new", too.

And people are ALWAYS on the lookout for new (we are "hard wired" to respond to it).

The good news is, just by following the strategies in this book you will (in many cases) be naturally doing the opposite of everyone else. While your competition is trying to con, coax and wrestle people into buying, you are simply tapping into psychological principles proven to work for   thousands of years.

Whatever the case, look at how your competitors are selling and test doing the exact *opposite*.

It's a great way to arrest attention (Crackerjack Selling Secret #40) and position yourself (Crackerjack Selling Secret #22) as different.

Crackerjack Selling Secret #67:
Spinning "No's" Into Gold

Back in the middle ages there used to be tales about *alchemists*—people who claimed to be able to turn worthless metals (like *lead*) into valuable metals like *gold.*

Of course, nobody was really ever able to do it.

And today, alchemy is considered a fairy tale on the scale of elves, dwarves and hobbits. But, if you are trying to persuade people to buy your product or service, there is a way to use a special kind of alchemy to...

**Convert "Nos"
Into "Yeses"**

Let me explain:

As you may have realized, most people HATE to tell other people no.

It's one of the main reasons why so few people enjoy talking to sales people at all. They don't want to tell them no (which is yet another reason to take <u>Crackerjack Selling Secret #6</u> to heart—giving permission to say no right off the bat.)

Anyway, here is the point:

When someone tells you no, or says they have no interest in buying because they can't afford it or simply don't want it, there is one last thing you can try. It's a long shot. And it won't always work. In fact, it's a lot like the quarterback throwing a 40-yard touchdown pass. And like that pass, if it works...

**You Can Still Pull
Out a "Win"**

And that is, when you are told no, you simply say something like, "I completely understand your decision. I was wondering, however, if you know of anyone else who might be interested?"

Now, usually one or two things will happen:

1. They will say they don't know anyone

2. They will actually give you the name of one or more people

Sometimes this will be because they feel bad they didn't buy. Or they really DO know someone who would be interested. Either way, you can often ask for something else—such as a referral—if you ask right when they deny you.

There's certainly no harm in asking, is there?

And who knows?

The people they refer you to could turn into your best customers down the road.

Crackerjack Selling Secret #68:
Give 'em Hell

I'll never forget this great sales lesson I learned (as a *customer*) many years ago.

I don't even remember what the "thing" was being sold (I think it was a tool of some kind).

But I do remember it was expensive and I was on the "fence" about buying. I just couldn't make up my mind. And I had listened to the presentation (which was on a video) all the way through, credit card half way out the whole time.

Then, at the end, the speaker "got" me. What he said was (paraphrased),

> *"Look, I know this is expensive. It's not cheap as we don't sell cheaply made products. And so, before deciding, please consider this: The worst that can happen is you buy it, use it for the next 30 days however you like and if isn't everything we have promised, or if you are not happy with it for any reason, even if you just don't like the color, let us know and we will return your money with no questions asked. You will have gotten to use the product free and are out maybe a little time using it. If you can't live with that then, please, do NOT buy it. On the other hand..."*

Now, on the surface, it seems like the guarantee (which is common in many industries today) closed the deal.

But it didn't. Not entirely, at least. No, the real power here was in the...

"Worst Case" Scenario.

Showing people the hellish, *worst* case scenario—which isn't really that bad, and can be spun into something GOOD—can be extremely persuasive.

There are many reasons why this works so well.

One of the big ones is it makes people feel *safe* buying from you. It also shows you truly do *care* about them (Crackerjack Selling Secret #1)—as you are being honest and forthright. You aren't saying the product is perfect (nothing is) and are in that sense admitting a flaw (Crackerjack Selling Secret #12).

Bottom line:

Show the "hell" side of buying, and you can make it much *easier* to buy from you.

Crackerjack Selling Secret #69:
Trick Your competition into Doing Your Selling for You

As we saw in <u>Crackerjack Selling Secret #38</u>, your offer can make or break everything.

And as much as us sales types LOVE to attribute success to our presentation and marketing skills...

**The *Offer* Can Many Times
Carry the Sale On Its Own!**

But what we haven't talked about is specifically *how* to structure an offer.

You see, one of the best ways to sell your product—assuming you really do have the "goods"—is to offer a "brass balls" guarantee. And one reliable way to do so is to say:

"If you aren't convinced this product/service is the best choice,
I'll buy you my competitor's product/service."

You can't get *gutsier* than that.

It's like tricking your competition into doing your selling FOR you (without them even knowing it). And it's that kind of raging confidence in your product or service that makes it very difficult for people to NOT want to buy from you. I first saw this a few years ago when helping a client sell his martial arts classes. Instead of the standard free offer or guarantee, we said if they aren't happy, we'll buy them a month of classes at any other local martial arts school of their choosing.

Did it work?

Oh Yeah, Baby!

And we never got *anyone* taking us up on the offer, either.

In fact, if you have a truly valuable product or service, you have nothing to worry about. Most people aren't looking to rip you off. Most people just want to feel *secure* in their purchase—that your product or service really does work as promised.

And using this Crackerjack Selling secret makes that buying decision a "no brainer."

Crackerjack Selling Secret #70:
How to Recruit Help from Master Sales Pros

One great way to get good—really *good*—at selling, is to observe how you feel and what you're thinking when YOU are persuaded to buy something.

And then *duplicate* whatever it was that "worked" on you.

Just take note whenever you are persuaded to buy and then "tap" into that same emotion, feeling and the *words* used. What questions did the sales person ask? What was the offer? How was it worded? What were you feeling at the time? How did the sales pro counter your objections? And most important of all...

What Made You
Buy This Thing?

And then write it down in a notebook or on your computer.

By regularly doing this (literally taking *notes* with pencil and paper on whatever made you buy) you sort of "recruit" the help of other, master sales professionals. And you will start making all kinds of wonderful sales discoveries.

Discoveries you can many times use when selling to *your* customers.

Crackerjack Selling Secret #71:
Tap Their Inner Laziness

Like it or not, most people are pretty lazy.

I know I can be. And so is just about everyone else I have ever known. I mean let's face it, most people would rather not have to do work, than to do work. It's just the way we are, I guess. However, this isn't an entirely bad thing. In fact, when it comes to sales...

**You Can Use Laziness
To Your Advantage!**

How?

It's easy:

Just explain to your prospects how there will never be an easier and more *convenient* time to buy what you are selling than right NOW. In other words, if they wait, it will be much more expensive. Or, they will have to wait in a line and check in constantly to see if there are any more available. Or, the next time what you are selling is offered, they will be competing with a bunch of people who will already possess your product, making it much harder to compete (works especially well for business-to-business type products/services).

And so on and so forth.

The point here is to make people realize it will be more "work" to buy or use what you are selling later than it is now. This way, not only do you up the chances of making the sale, but you are doing them a real service at the same time.

And as a result, everyone wins.

Crackerjack Selling Secret #72:
Mr. Spock's Super Sales Secret

Chances are you have (at some point) watched the old *Star Trek* shows.

And you may remember how the ever-logical Mr. Spock persuaded ("sold") the good captain Kirk to do certain things and follow his advice.

Well, guess what?

There is a way to apply one of *Mr. Spock's* persuasion secrets to *your* selling. And that is by injecting into your sales and marketing presentations what marketing genius Eugene Schwartz called:

"The Language of Logic"

What is the language of logic?

It's words and phrases that carry an air of logic, reason and even *science* behind them. Such as words or expressions you'd hear in a courtroom, a lab or from a textbook. Words and phrases like:

- In test after test

- Science shows

- Research proves

- Reasonably

- But the fact remains

- That is a fact

- Incidentally

- Irrefutable

The idea here is to pepper these types of "smart" quotes in your presentations—especially when talking about big claims that sound *unbelievable*. Plus, by using words or phrases people automatically associate with truth and logic, you tone down the "hype" part of the claim, and make it more easily believed.

Here's a real-life example of this in an ad selling a money-making product (a very skeptical market):

> *"Instead, these experts discovered—what savvy businessmen still know today—the best way to make a lot of money very fast is to simply 'leverage' off other people's time, efforts, resources and money."*

See what I mean?

Words like "leverage" and phrases like "these experts discovered" temper the claim about making money fast—making it more believable and easier to accept. This is another one of the more "tactical" secrets in this book.

And it is *especially* effective when used with written sales (ads, sales letters, etc.).

Crackerjack Selling Secret #73:
Watch-Wearer's Advantage

"It is my conviction that a person who cannot keep appointments on time, cannot keep scheduled commitments, or cannot stick to a schedule cannot be trusted in other ways either."

-Dan Kennedy
"No BS Time Management"
Page 39

Although most people never think about it, if you want to be *instantly* more trusted (and therefore make more sales—Crackerjack Selling Secret #1), all you sometimes have to do is be where you say you're going to be, when you say you're going to be there, at all times with no exceptions, period. Fact is, many people put MUCH more trust in those who do what they say, at the time they say they'll do it, without excuses.

Maybe it's because it's so rare?

Or because it shows you have *respect* for the other person's time (which is also rare in today's overly narcissistic world)?

Whatever the case, if you want to be better at selling...

Show Up on Time.

Be there when you say you will arrive. Call when you say you will call. Show up where you say you will show up, and on time. Do this and people will know you place value on their time. That you care at *least* that much more about them. And will feel much better about buying from you (even if they aren't consciously *thinking* about it).

This is probably the *simplest* Crackerjack Selling Secret in this book.

And all you need is a watch and/or an alarm clock to "use" it.

Crackerjack Selling Secret #74:
Butt into the Conversation

This is another great selling secret that, while originated by a direct mail copywriter, can be directly applied to *any* kind of selling.

Here's the scoop:

Back in the early 1900's, there lived a brilliant mail order copywriter named Robert Collier. Robert's book, *The Robert Collier Letter Book* is an advertising "cult classic" that—even today, almost 100 years later—is used by copywriters around the world. And besides the dozens of great advertising and sales psychology examples in the book, the most widely quoted part is:

**"Enter the conversation
already going on
in the customer's head."**

In other words... when you are trying to sell someone something figure out what that person is thinking about *now* and "step" into that internal conversation.

What thoughts are constantly *racing* through their minds?

What *fears* are they worried about?

What do they secretly *want* more than anything (Crackerjack Selling Secret #2) and what does it have to do with what they are thinking about right NOW?

Answer those questions and...

Selling Gets Easy!

This is why so many of the best sales and marketing experts recommend keeping up with current events in the world and tying those events into what you sell. What *news* stories are hot? What's going on in your customer's *industry*? What *trends* are happening in your customer's world? The answers to these questions (and in face-to-face sales, you need only ask) are important before trying to sell someone something—whether in person, print, online or even over the phone.

Remember Robert Collier's famous line and you will never go wrong.

Crackerjack Selling Secret #75:
How to Make it Hard to Tell You "no"

Remember <u>Crackerjack Selling Secret #67</u> when we talked about how people don't like to say "no" to other people? Well, here's another way to use this reality to your advantage:

Make your requests *reasonable*.

In other words, at every stage of your selling, make the commitments easy and even...

Pleasant.

Fact is, most people will NOT tell you no if your requests are reasonable. That's why coming up with powerful offers (<u>Crackerjack Selling Secret #38</u>) is so important.

For example, isn't it easier for someone to agree to your requests by saying something like, "Please, do not make up your mind now. Take this widget home and use it for the weekend and THEN decide"? Not only would that "try it before they buy it" offer let you use the awesome power of *demonstration* (<u>Crackerjack Selling Secret #11</u>), but it's easy to say "yes" to. Another way to use this secret is to only get the other person to commit to answering a few of your questions: "May I ask a question?" "Would it be okay if I asked you something?" "I have another question, if that would be okay."

All of which lets you start the sales off on the right foot—asking questions (<u>Crackerjack Selling Secret #3</u>) and finding out what their pains and desires are (<u>Crackerjack Selling Secret #2</u>).

There are actually a lot of ways to be reasonable in selling.

And the more reasonable your requests...

**The More Successful
You'll Be!**

Doing so not only makes it *easy* for people to say yes but, when your requests are truly reasonable, it actually makes it *difficult* for people to say no.

Crackerjack Selling Secret #76:
Be A Multi-Cultural Warrior

One of the best sales books (actually, it was an eBook) ever written is from the late, brilliant copywriter and marketer Gary Halbert.

It is called:

**"Gary Halbert's Guide to the Core Secrets and Desires
Of Different Groups of People and How to Exploit
Those Secrets and Desires to Make Yourself a Lot of Money!"**

And "politically incorrect" as it sounds—it reveals the hidden hot buttons of over 31 different kinds of people—including different ethnicities, professions and age groups.

I've read this eBook probably 15 times and STILL get something new from it every time.

But the most useful thing I got from it was realizing there is indeed a difference between the way people of different cultures and backgrounds...

**Make their
Buying Decisions.**

For example:

In some cases, people of different races and cultures have completely different life experiences and "hot buttons" that motivate, scare, anger or turn them off from wanting to buy. And the same goes for different *professions*, too. Like executives (this one REALLY shocked me when I read it), policemen, dentists, government workers, sales people, entrepreneurs—all have different core desires in a lot of cases.

Anyway, here's the point:

As politically incorrect as it may seem, if you want to become a truly great sales pro...

**You Have to Look
At the World As It IS.**

Not as the "talking heads" wish it was.

Like it or not, lawyers really do respond differently to sales messages than nurses. People of different cultures and backgrounds often have completely different buying patterns and habits. Older people respond WAY differently to sales messages than younger people, etc.

The point?

Get to learn and know the cultural, occupational and social backgrounds of your customers and prospects. What are their *biases*? What are their *unique* pains? Get to know... really KNOW... people at this level and...

**You Will Automatically
Ratchet Up More Sales!**

It takes lots of observation and study. But it's worth its weight in *gold*.

Plus, this ties in directly to Crackerjack Selling Secret #41—if you find you simply cannot identify (and be honest with yourself if this is the case) with a certain racial, demographic or occupational group you want to sell to—find someone who *does* identify with them to do the sales presentation.

This will go a LONG way towards helping you sell more.

Crackerjack Selling Secret #77:
The Dear Abby Persuasion Formula

I don't know if this is always true, but I have heard that, after the comics, the most read section of the average newspaper is the "Dear Abby" column. Whether that's true or not, there's no doubt millions of people read columns on advice, relationships, etc. And, if you pay attention to certain magazines, you will notice a lot of ads are now structured like "advice" columns instead of ads.

Why?

Because This Format Just
Flat Out Works!

Believe it or not, some of the most persuasive selling is now done "Q&A" style.

On the Internet, a health and fitness expert named Matt Furey does this in his emails all the time. So does financial author Dave Ramsey. I do it often when writing emails to my subscribers, as well, and it works like crazy.

Anyway, here's my point:

If you can re-position your selling as a "Q&A"—something that offers advice, which people are *conditioned* to trust and *enjoy* hearing—you can often persuade more people to buy from you.

This is a no-brainer if you are using written forms of persuasion (emails, sales letters, Internet audio or video, etc.). But you can also do this with tele-seminars and even *public speaking*. One public speaking expert I know recommends grabbing a stool and answering audience questions while subtly selling your products in the answers.

Whatever you sell, try it and see what happens.

It can many times make a big difference in your overall profits.

Crackerjack Selling Secret #78:
Hollywood's Best-Kept Sales Secret

Back in college, I used to want to be a screenwriter. Not sure why exactly... but I really wanted to write movie scripts. I even once wrote a detailed research paper on the subject. And one of the big lessons I learned during that research was that, in a movie, your main character MUST have a purpose or a "mission." The screenwriting books called it:

"A Motivation"

The more intense and driven the motivation, the *better* the story is almost every time.

It's the same with *selling*, too.

If you have a mission—a vision—for your customers, product, industry (and even the world itself) you will be *naturally* more persuasive. People are literally *drawn* to other people with a purpose and a passion for accomplishing a goal. We sense that energy and want to be a *part* of it. And that's why, if you show you have a real purpose and vision for what you sell—and let your customers know about it—you will *automatically* sell more by your sheer, relentless energy.

People will be *drawn* to you.

This explains why people who pursue their passions—and not just "the money"—tend to do so well. Because we have a purpose beyond just money and people *feel* it. And in many cases they even want to be a *part* of it.

Even if it means *buying* from you to do so.

Crackerjack Selling Secret #79:
How to Get Customers to Sell Themselves on Buying From You

One thing people hate is to be told, "you're wrong!"

If you want to make absolutely sure you turn someone off, and create a situation that is impossible to sell in, simply tell someone they are wrong.

Unfortunately, a lot of people do this.

If a customer or prospect has an objection or is misinformed and says something that is totally wrong and inaccurate, the businessman's natural reaction—since he usually does have the facts and data—is to say the customer is wrong. Which usually just causes an argument (or at least some tension) and...

Costs Them the Sale.

So, what should you do instead?

The key is to let other people reach the right conclusion on their *own*.

And the best way to do that is to use Crackerjack Selling Secret #3—ask questions.

Instead of saying someone is wrong, ask something like, "Look, I may be wrong, but isn't it true that...?" Or, "Okay, Mr. Prospect, I understand, I have heard that as well. Here's what I think....now tell me where I'm going wrong here." Or, "I could be wrong about that, you may very well be right and that's fine, so let's take another look at the facts to make sure I'm on the right page here..."

See how that works?

If you want to ethically persuade someone—and not *manipulate*—you simply ask questions. Make others look at the facts as they are. And ask them in a way that ultimately creates *vision* (Crackerjack Selling Secret #4) so they feel they discovered the facts for themselves.

It all goes back to asking questions.

Most selling is not done by the salesman or marketers. It's done by the customer... to *themselves*.

123

Crackerjack Selling Secret #80:
The Best Salesmen to Study

Here's another sales tip that's easy to implement. And while it may seem odd at first, you can start using it immediately just by turning on your television set or checking your email!

Anyway, here it is:

**Observe Those Who
Are *Bad* At Selling!**

Why would you want to do this?

Because in many cases, learning what works is simply a matter of doing what does NOT work. If you observe people who are not good at sales—or who use shady "tricks"—you can get a good idea of what NOT to do.

I'm serious about this, too.

Next time someone tries to sell you something in a way that turns you off, "bottle" that moment up.

Meditate on it.

And, make sure you *never* do what they did.

Are they being pushy? Are they trying to manipulate you with one-liners and fancy "closes"? Are they reciting company propaganda without letting you get a word in edge-wise? Do they get *defensive* if you ask questions or raise objections? Are they just spewing hype and nonsense? Are they even *trying* to back up their claims? What is it about what they are doing that is *repulsing* you? This may seem obvious, at first. But you may be surprised by how many things you are doing that annoy and repel customers by observing the salesmen that annoy and repel you. And if you find you ARE doing any of these things, you can increase your sales just by ceasing to do them anymore.

Crackerjack Selling Secret #81:
If You Want Someone to Do What You Want...

Earlier I mentioned the great persuader Gerry Spence (Crackerjack Selling Secret #5). And how you can learn a lot about selling from his books, stories and especially his take on *preparation*.

Here's another nugget of Gerry Spence gold from, *How to Argue And Win Every Time*:

> **"Winning [an argument] is getting what we want,**
> **which often includes assisting**
> **others in getting what they want."**

Of course, this is nothing new.

But its importance cannot be overstated.

This is why you will see ads offering free reports, books, videos, etc., BEFORE trying to sell or pitch you anything. It is why the best salesmen really do take the time to *care* about their customer (Crackerjack Selling Secret #1)—to figure out what their pain is and what they want—and then show them how to get the solution.

In a lot of ways, selling is more like "assisting" than it is "selling."

This is why giving free consultations (Crackerjack Selling Secret #64), for example, work so well. They make it easy for someone to do some favor back to you. And usually in the form of...

Buying What You Got!

Moral of the story?

Before asking something of someone, help them *first*. That way you set the law of reciprocity into motion.

And with that massive wind at your back, your selling gets much easier.

Crackerjack Selling Secret #82:
The Most Powerful Question You Can Ask in Sales

One of my favorite business books is Ken McCarthy's System Club Letters.

This is a compilation of letters Ken wrote to his "System Club" members (the most prestigious Internet marketing club in the world). And it contains all kinds of priceless business tips and advice. One tip that stands out like a sore thumb is his chapter about how most businesses have...

"Customer De-motivation
Departments"

In other words, they have employees who act like weeds in a garden—who start out small and hidden. But soon start growing all over the place and destroying all the good plants around them. His example was how he tried to order an iPod but the website was not working and there was no other way to order.

The result?

A $200+ sale blown because they didn't make it easy to order and act.

As you can imagine, there is a huge selling lesson here.

And that is, at the end of the day in sales, many times half the "battle" is simply...

Making It Easier to Say
"Yes!" Than "No"!

This is so powerful, I'll even go so far as to say this:

If you make it a goal (in whatever you are selling) to make buying from you easier than NOT buying, you almost can't lose. This is why doing things like matching a perfect product to what your prospects desperately want (Crackerjack Selling Secret #2) is so important.

What can you do to make it easier to buy than NOT to buy?

Ask yourself this question and write down whatever comes to mind.

Trust me, if you do this, you will come up with all kinds of ways to "sweeten" your deals, remove obstacles (you may have quite a few and not realize it), re-educate employees, and a hundred other things that can quickly put more money in your pocket.

Best part?

This is one of those things none of your competition will likely ever think to do.

Crackerjack Selling Secret #83:
The Proof Is in the Pudding

Proof.

This one little word is the "rock" that holds up all sales. Gary Bencivenga—considered the world's top copywriter and a master salesman—considers this THE key to persuasion if you read his ezine at www.BencivengaBullets.com.

And he doesn't get much argument about it, either.

When we see the solution to a problem, pain or desire, we naturally have an almost desperate want to believe it's true. But *saying* you have the solution...

Is No Longer Enough!

It may have been back in the day before there was so much selling and marketing going on (statistics show the average person is bombarded by OVER 3,000 persuasive messages per day).

Now you have to *prove* your case if you want people to believe you.

And if you want to quickly and easily sell more, simply prove what you say is true. Ask yourself questions like, how can I back up my claims? Who else uses my product or service? What do THEY say about it? What research and statistics do I have? What media has endorsed me? (Crackerjack Selling Secret #15.) What authorities or celebrities have given me their "seal of approval"? (Crackerjack Selling Secret #18.) What would I have to say to convince a fair-minded jury what I am claiming about my product and service (and what it will DO for my customer) is true beyond a shadow of a doubt?

Fact is, nobody buys if they don't actually *believe* what you're saying.

And the best way to get someone to believe you is to use things like gaining their trust (Crackerjack Selling Secret #1), preparation (Crackerjack Selling Secret #5), getting endorsed by experts (Crackerjack Selling Secret #52), telling stories about other people who used your product or service (Crackerjack Selling Secret #9) and any other ways you can *prove* what you say.

Always ask yourself—with every claim or promise—how can you prove your case?

Because even if you don't ask this question, you can be assured that's what your customers are asking as they hear your pitch.

Crackerjack Selling Secret #84:
Make 'Em Stars

This secret is the brother to <u>Crackerjack Selling Secret #9</u>—telling stories.

You see, it's one thing to just tell stories. It's quite another to tell a story that helps you *sell*.

And one extremely powerful way to tell persuasive stories is to tell a story where...

Your Customers
Are the *Stars*.

In other words, putting your customer *in* the story—so they can mentally *experience* the benefits and advantages of what you are selling. This is a great way to sell often used in old direct marketing ads.

It is also easily used in any other kind of selling.

The idea is to put your customer in the "story" using the product or service—as other people approve (<u>Crackerjack Selling Secret #18</u>), as they enjoy the benefits and even as other people they know come to them for "advice" about whatever it is your customer can now do.

Very powerful psychology at work here.

Especially if you're thoroughly prepared (<u>Crackerjack Selling Secret #5</u>) and really *know* what your customers desperately *want* (<u>Crackerjack selling secret #2</u>). The idea is to put them in the story—like "stars" in their own movie—and let them experience what you sell (even if only through their imagination) and "own" it in their minds.

Some of the best sales presentations you will ever see do this.

It's not only 100% ethical (and even *entertaining* for people), but also extremely effective.

Crackerjack Selling Secret #85:
Listen to The Bitchin'

Let's face it:

We sales and entrepreneurial-minded people tend to be optimistic—with super-charged, "out of the way, we're coming through!" attitudes. Heck, we HAVE to be this way. And because of this, many of us shy away from anything negative.

But guess what?

In some ways this kind of thinking (if left "unchecked")...

**Can Kill
Your Sales!**

Especially when it comes to listening to the negativity of your *customers*. I'm not saying to embrace negative thinking or anything like that. What I am saying is, to openly encourage your customers to *vent* their anger. Whether it be about you and your product, or someone else's.

Why?

Because when you take the time to listen to your customers' complaints, they often times:

1. *Trust* you more because you are actually LISTENING to them. (Don't we all just want to be heard?)

2. Will tell you *exactly* what you need in order to sell them your product or service (or *keep* them as a customer).

In fact, an angry, venting customer will tell you all kinds of things about what they want, what problems they need solved, and what they must hear from you before buying. This goes back to asking questions (Crackerjack Selling Secret #3). And is why instead of hiding from your customer complaints you should almost...

Encourage Them!

Hear them out. You'll be doing them AND yourself a huge service.

And increase your sales at the same time.

Crackerjack Selling Secret #86:
Take A Big, Wet "Bite" Out of Selling

As you may or may not know, people are "wired" to listen to news.

Human beings are "built" with a special sensor that makes us always on the lookout for news. It's a great survival mechanism that kept our ancestors alive a few thousand years ago (such as when a predator was roaming around)... and is still with us today. That's why ads and other selling messages with a news "flavor" to them often do extremely well. Especially these days, when people are *showered* with sales pitches daily.

And one great way to ethically sell is to simply make your communications with your customers more "newsy."

How?

The answer is simple:

Use Sound Bites!

Sound bites are basically short, "newsy" quotes that turn otherwise long (sometimes REALLY long) messages into easy-to-repeat, memorable phrases.

And if you want to both 1.) Sound "newsy" and 2.) Make what you say *impossible* for your customers to forget... then peppering your sales presentations with great sound bites is a must. You see politicians use them all the time. Most of us can't keep track of all the lies that spew out of the average politician's mouth. But we sure do remember his (or her) *sound bites*, don't we?

Now here's the thing:

Creating sound bites is definitely more an "art" than a "science". And I wish I had a magic wand that'd instantly teach you how to create them. But until I find one, the best way for you to get the "knack" of creating sound bites is to read and listen to good sound bites, and then practice creating your own.

Obviously, I can't do the practicing part for you.

But I can give you a dozen or so examples of great sound bites you can study, model and adapt for your own purposes. Simply read through them regularly and ask how you can apply them to your product or service? Before long, you'll be coming up with your own sound bites.

Anyway, without further ado, here are the sample sound bites:

It's like giving your dog a loaded gun and letting him play Russian Roulette!

One will learn more by spending $1,000 at Amazon and reading for six months than by spending $150,000 and four years at an Ivy League university. (From *political columnist Vox Day.)*

Might as well throw your kids on the grill now! (From a press release about chimney cleaning written by Livtar Khalsa of "Conscious Cleaning Chimney Service")

You might as well just feed our dog rat poison and cyanide now! (My adaption for a dog product)

Most people are too busy earning a living to make any money. (Deck copy to the famous Joe Karbo "Lazy Man's Way To Riches" ad)

One lawyer with a briefcase can steal more than a thousand thieves with guns. (From the book, "How to Out Fox The Foxes")

A consultant is someone who can tell you 300 ways to make love, but can't get a date on Friday night.

Parasites have killed more humans than all the wars in history! (From Gary Halbert's "Ultimate Colon Cleansing" ad)

For every illness, there is a country where it simply doesn't exist. (From copywriter Jim Rutz's "Read This or Die" ad).

Okay, those are a just a handful of sound bites to get you started.

Now, at first, you may wonder if what you wrote is really a decent sound bite or not. If you find yourself in that spot, just ask yourself:

**"Would this make a great quote on a radio
or TV show, or in a newspaper or magazine?"**

In other words, if it sounds "news worthy", then you got yourself a good sound bite. If it sounds like "selling" then you probably don't.

That's a nice, simple way of judging the quality of your sound bites.

Crackerjack Selling Secret #87:
How to Use the Laws of Physics to Sell More

One BIG sales mistake a lot of people make is being pushy. *Nobody* likes a pushy salesman. And yet, so many salesman are pushy.

Why?

I don't know.

But in some ways, the laws of physics apply to selling: When you push a ball in any direction, it tends to roll away from you. And your customers do the *same* thing: When you try to "push" the sale, they *recoil*, the sales defenses go up, and you're pretty much...

Out of Luck!

So one Crackerjack Selling Secret to keep in mind from here on out is simply don't push.

And if you do have to push (and sometimes we must), make sure you attach a rope around them so, like a yo-yo, they come back. By that I mean, don't tell people, "You NEED to have this gun—it will protect you and your family!" Instead, proceed it with an "If" statement combined with vision (Crackerjack Selling Secret #4).

> *"If you don't want your wife or kids to spend a night in the emergency room or worse, then you may want to consider getting a good firearm."*

See how that works?

Whether verbally or writing, use "If/then" statements.

Not only does the very structure of it help build credibility, but it buffers the "hard edge" pushing most customers hate and run away from.

Crackerjack Selling Secret #88:
The Secret of Selling with Your Hands

You might find this hard to believe, but back in the olden days, promoters used to try "hypnotizing" customers and prospects with their hands. Many claimed they could put people into trances and persuade them to buy what they were selling.

Personally, I don't believe it.

Even so, there is definitely one proven way to use your hands to persuade people to buy in a totally legal, ethical and moral way.

And that is by using...

Handwritten Letters!

It's absolutely true, too.

If you REALLY want to get someone's attention (Crackerjack Selling Secret #40)... and *keep* their attention... there is no better way than by cranking out a *handwritten* letter.

Think about it:

Have you ever tossed out a handwritten letter before reading it? I know I haven't. In fact, direct mailers have known for *years* if you can send someone a direct mail piece in a handwritten envelope, your chances of having it opened go up *exponentially*. These same people have also discovered if you can somehow simulate handwriting (such as with special fonts) you can...

Drive Your Sales
Through the *Roof.*

If there's a customer you really want to sell to, test using a *handwritten* letter.

Not only is it guaranteed to be read and paid attention to... but it can also significantly ratchet up your chances of making the sale.

After all, how can you NOT give a personal, handwritten letter your complete attention?

Crackerjack Selling Secret #89:
How to Get People *Looking* for Reasons to Buy

Not long ago, I got a sales letter that—while extremely well written and selling a very

high-quality product—committed a truly stupid sales mistake. A mistake that happens all the time no just in copywriting sales—but in all kinds of selling. A mistake that probably cost the company running the ad a TON of money.

What was this mistake?

Well, in order to make a point, it blatantly insulted the "Intelligent Design" movement—saying people who believed it were misguided and not too "intelligent."

Okay so what?

Well, this debate—no matter what side you are on—is erupting around the U.S.

And if you look at any poll, you will see at least half the people in the U.S.—and even a

good chunk of people in more secular countries, like the United Kingdom—don't believe in random evolution. Which means, unless he was writing to atheists, humanists or other people who do not believe in intelligent design (he was writing to people who are interested in making money—which spans almost every group of people), he *automatically* turned away people who disagree with him, by smugly violating their established belief systems.

And in the process...

Murdered a Good Portion
of His Sales!

How?

Because when you say something that violates someone's core beliefs—whether you're right or wrong (it makes no difference)—instead of looking for reasons to buy from you, people will start to look for reasons NOT to buy from you.

Even if they want what you have.

And even if they *need* it.

That doesn't mean you will lose everyone. And in some cases (such as if you are writing to your own list or only want to attract people who believe exactly as you) it can be smart. But you will almost always lose people (maybe even a *lot* of people) who would otherwise have bought from you.

And these lost sales can add up real fast.

Even Hollywood is finally catching on to this. Films and TV shows that star the more "outspoken" actors—especially the ones who used to bring in tens of millions of moviegoers—are now flopping left and right. This is even the case when the movie is good and has lots of publicity. On the other hand—and again, Hollywood is finally learning this lesson—if you say things that *reinforce* and *agree* with your customer's beliefs, then they will be more willing to hear you out and listen.

All of which can make a big difference in your results.

Crackerjack Selling Secret #90:
Silence the Skeptics

Weird as it sounds, sometimes—and this is especially true when you are selling an extremely well-constructed product or service, with lots of testimonials and huge results—you can almost get "trapped" by your product's power.

But that I mean, we truly do live in the "age of skepticism."

And a lot of people are quick to ignore outrageous claims...

Even If They Are *True!*

Which means, when you are selling something that really does "walk the walk", you have to be even *more* careful talking about all the wonderful claims and advantages your product has. Everyone has very sensitive "bs meters" right now. Everyone from our preachers and teachers to the media and our politicians are lying to us left and right.

So, what do you do?

Luckily, there are lots of things you can do. Just following the psychological principles in this book will usually help carry you over this particular "hump." Such as having solid positioning (Crackerjack Selling Secret #22), celebrity status (Crackerjack Selling secret #15), strong authority (Crackerjack Selling Secret #52), and proof (Crackerjack selling secret #83).

But even so, you can also play the... "I know this is crazy, but..." card.

What that means is, whenever you say something that could be taken as hype or some kind of wild-haired claim that cannot be true... instead of ignoring it, hiding it or hoping your prospects don't think of it... you instead...

Acknowledge It!

In other words... say something like:

"Hey, I KNOW this sounds almost like BS, but..."

Or... "Sounds almost crazy, doesn't it? I understand, but here's what we found..."

See how that works?

You validate the question going on in your prospects' minds. It makes what you say more believable and likely to be heard. And it doesn't sound like you are insulting their intelligence.

All of which goes a long way towards bumping your sales.

Crackerjack Selling Secret #91:
Use Skepticism to Your Advantage

Let's talk more about natural customer *skepticism*.

But this time, instead of trying to get rid of your customer's natural, reasonable and *understandable* skepticism... let's talk about how to use it...

To Your Advantage!

Here's how:

A lot of times, selling can be made much less frustrating if you but assume your customers are hard core skeptics and act accordingly. However, because sales people are by nature so optimistic and good buyers ourselves (many of us are borderline *suckers* for a good pitch), we tend to forget the rest of the world is skeptical.

And how they think everything we're saying is a bald-faced *lie*.

So if you switch gears and approach selling as if everyone is a skeptic—and literally thinking (if not *saying*) "I don't believe a word of this, you are insulting my intelligence"—you will say and do things quite differently, wouldn't you? Like dig up more authority and credibility (Crackerjack Selling Secret #53). Seek out more proof for your case (Crackerjack Selling Secret #83). Work harder on your positioning (Crackerjack Selling Secret #22). Ask the right kind of questions (Crackerjack Selling Secret #3).

And so on, and so forth.

Remember, Crackerjack Selling is NOT about pulling out a magic sales "technique" or dazzling your customers with some souped-up "close." It's about using sound psychological principles that have withstood the test of time in thousands of selling situations.

Go with the "flow" of how your customer *already* wants information delivered.

That way you can make sales much easier with less effort.

Crackerjack Selling Secret #92:
Study the Rags—Make More Sales

You may have noticed I've been saying the name "Eugene Schwartz" quite a bit.

And one of the biggest "ah ha!" moments about selling I ever got was when he gave a speech to a giant direct mail company called *Phillips Publishing*. He dropped a *ton* of great sales tips and advice during that speech. The one that sticks out most in my mind is when he talked about the importance of reading "low culture" magazines, going to popular movies and watching popular TV shows.

His explanation is that doing those things lets you "tap" into what people are buying...

Right NOW!

What is *getting* people to go spend $10 and sit in a crowded theater packed with obnoxious teenagers and kids? What is *compelling* people to religiously watch certain TV shows week in and week out—without missing a beat? What *exactly* makes people sneak the *National Enquirer*, *Cosmo* and *Weekly World News* into their shopping cart when nobody is watching?

Gene called this the "under culture"—the hidden benefits, ideas and appeals people are almost ashamed to talk about and admit.

But if (for example) you understand *why* people love watching movies about laser swords and space ships (despite the terrible acting and plot holes)...

You Can Use that
Intelligence in
YOUR Selling!

Because you will understand *nobody* is "squeaky clean."

That what people SAY they want to buy is not always what they WILL buy.

And that their belief "threshold" may be larger (or smaller) than you might think.

This is why it can be so profitable to participate in the under-culture. To know what people are passionately talking about at the water cooler. And to read what they are reading...

When Nobody Is *Looking*.

Low culture contains the "hidden benefits" and appeals your customers may be looking for.

Know them, and take your sales to a whole new level.

Crackerjack Selling Secret #93:
The Titillating Ghosts Strategy

As we saw in **Crackerjack Selling Secret #83**—the average person (including you and me) is bombarded by over 3,000 sales messages per day.

And that's actually an *older* statistic.

It's probably MUCH more than that, now.

These messages take the form of everything from billboards to pop-up ads to TV commercials and everything in between. *Everyone's* trying to sell us. And in Crackerjack Selling Secret #88 we talked about how the first "battle" of the sales war is simply getting attention. Well, to piggyback on that, let's talk about the next "battle" you have to win:

KEEPING Your
Customer's Attention!

How do you keep someone's attention?

A lot of it comes from knowing your customers (Crackerjack Selling Secret #2) and asking the right questions (Crackerjack Selling Secret #3). But from a *tactical* point of view—you want to simply make it easier to *keep* listening to you than to *stop* listening to you.

In other words, you cannot "bore" people into buying.

But you can *fascinate* and *titillate* them into buying. You can keep their flagging interest by dialing in your every word to their wants, needs, fears and desires—so they have no choice but to cling to your every word.

So ALWAYS be asking yourself questions like:

"What can I say that is life or death important to my customer?" "What is the ONE thing I can say right now that will make it impossible for my customer to ignore me?" "How can I make sure they have no *choice* but to keep listening?"

A lot of this comes from observation and asking questions.

For example, the great marketer Jim Rutz once talked about a school teacher trying to keep her students' attention when reading them stories. One day she realized whenever she talked about ghosts...

Her Students
Perked Up!

And so, from that point onward, no matter what story she told them, if she noticed their attention spans drifting, she'd throw a ghost in the story and recapture their attention.

This is how connected you want to be to your customers.

Because once you figure out what titillates them like that, you will find yourself giving sales presentations—in person, print, phone or whatever—that are far more compelling.

Crackerjack Selling Secret #94:
Crack the Consistency Code

Here's a cool little sales tip:

People LOVE to be consistent.

A lot of people tend to love routine and maps and "guidelines." Many of us would probably go bonkers without checklists. And we all tend to get VERY uncomfortable when our beliefs are challenged and don't make sense (which leads to another phenomenon called "cognitive dissonance"—Crackerjack Selling Secret #10).

So, what does that mean for your sales?

A LOT.

Because you can use this quirk of human nature to your advantage. And you do it by simply making sure everything you say...

Makes "Sense"

That it's logical.

And that you use language and examples that fall in line in your customer's mindset so there's no conflict or having to "think" about what you just said. This is why stories (Crackerjack Selling Secret #9) and parables (Crackerjack Selling Secret #27) work so well. They "line" things up in our minds and make even complicated concepts easily understood and...

Easy to *Agree* With.

When you are selling, stay consistent.

Make sure there are no "holes" in your arguments. And be sure you understand the objections that will be asked and how to make your answers "fit" into your customer's world (and not just some canned retort you read in some sales book).

Common sense?

Absolutely. But it's a powerful and important concept nonetheless. Stay logical and consistent in your points when selling and you will sell more.

Crackerjack Selling Secret #95:
Feed 'em Persuasion Candy

Once upon a time many years ago, I read a book about picking up women. It was mostly a dorky book full of false and naïve advice. However, it contained one bit of advice that was right smack on the money for selling.

It is actually related to Crackerjack Selling Secret #3 about asking questions.

But, with a "twist."

And that is to...

Validate What People
Are Feeling!

That doesn't mean you have to *agree* with them.

Just *validate* them.

And it makes a lot of sense, too. Don't we all just want to be heard? To be acknowledged? To have someone actually hear us out and take us seriously? Well, there is no better way to do all the above than by:

1. Listening to what your prospects say

2. And then "feeding" back what they just said

This could, I suppose, be considered a sales "trick." But it's not.

You are simply hearing them out and getting a good idea about what they *want* (Crackerjack Selling Secret #2). And then, when they are done, telling it all back to them. This naturally gives people the signal that you heard them out and, shock of shocks, CARE about what's important to them (Crackerjack Selling Secret #1). Which then prompts the other person to know you actually *heard* them. All of which makes people trust and like you more. As it means you really were paying attention and really do understand their concerns and wants.

This is like "persuasion candy."

And just about every top salesman I've ever learned from insists on doing it.

It's simple, powerful, and, if you want to make the maximum amount sales, *mandatory*.

Crackerjack Selling Secret #96:
Batman's Ginsu Knife Sales Attack

I don't know about you, but my all-time favorite movie is *Batman Begins*.

Not only because it's so entertaining and fun to watch... but also because of the many selling lessons in it. The most important of which is when Batman tells his butler (Alfred):

"People need dramatic examples
to shake them from their apathy."

So true.

So very, very, very true.

Most people are practically sleep walking through life. And it takes a lot of effort to engage and persuade the average person. One way to "wake them up" is by using powerful, dramatic examples. This not only helps arrest and keep attention (Crackerjack Selling Secrets #40 and #93), but it also makes your selling more effective.

Drama is an extremely powerful sales tool for anyone who sells anything for a living.

People are entertained and intrigued by dramatic examples.

That's why many people will often listen to or read certain sales pitches that detail how someone went from 300 pounds to 150 pounds by using a "secret weight loss method." Or why people will flock to MLM and other "business opportunities" based on a rags-to-riches story. Or why people will crowd around live demonstrations showing ordinary knives slicing through bricks, rocks and steel (remember those "Ginsu Knives"?)

It's all about the drama. Use it in your selling and...

A Whole New World
Will Open Up For You!

Instead of people falling asleep or getting bored, they will listen with wild-eyed enthusiasm and eagerness. The kind of excitement that leads to wallets being opened and customers that come back to you again and again and again—if for no other reason than the experience.

Crackerjack Selling Secret #97:
Hop on the Billion-Dollar Brand Wagon

* Jesus Christ * Oprah * Fidel Castro * Dr. Atkins * Donald Trump * Walt Disney * Karl Marx * Rush Limbaugh * Ronald McDonald * Adolf Hitler *

Pretty diverse list of people, ain't it?

And although some of these people are as opposite as chocolate and vanilla, they all have something in common. A powerful Crackerjack Selling tool you can use no matter what you sell or who you sell to.

And that is...

Personal Branding!

Now, I am not talking about the corporate, "Good Year Blimp" branding celebrated in Super Bowl commercials. *Personal* branding is quite different. Unlike the "image" branding—often built around a logo, blimp, song, etc.—personal branding is centered around a specific *person* (and personality). Think of that list of people above. Good, bad or ugly... they trigger *instant* name recognition and, in many cases, strong emotions.

You're usually either for or against them.

Heroes to some, villains to others.

And because of that, money (and sales) are...

Attracted Like Flies to Honey
To Them and Their Causes!

Think about it:

When you have the personal brand of a Rush Limbaugh, Marx, Oprah (or any of the people listed above)—no logo, blimp or song is needed to get people to remember you. All of which begs the question of *how* do you build an explosive personal brand? One that attracts people and cash to you like a magnet—keeping your business red-hot and automatically making your advertising even more effective?

It's actually pretty easy:

Just use the secrets in this book.

When you concentrate on actually *caring* about your customers (Crackerjack Selling Secret #1), using your personality (Crackerjack Selling Secret #56), getting media publicity (Crackerjack Selling Secret #15), securing top positioning (Crackerjack Selling Secret #22) and many of the other tips in this book, you will naturally build your own personal brand.

And sell many more dollars worth of your products and services at the same time.

For more details on how to do this, check out *The Brand Called You* by Peter Montoya.

Crackerjack Selling Secret #98:
Claim the "Cat-Bird" Seat

Remember Crackerjack Selling Secret #22 about positioning? How by JUST having good positioning, you can often outsell your competition (even if they are better "sellers") sometimes without even having to lift a finger?

Well, there is a certain place to position yourself where you almost can't help but be extremely successful.

It's sometimes called:

"The Catbird Seat"

Basically, this is a position in your market to where business flows naturally and easily.

It's like standing in front of a moving parade of customers and prospects who are flowing to you in such abundance you can't possibly serve them all.

And it's like positioning on *steroids*.

It is THE place to be in, when possible.

And probably the best way to nab it is to be the first (or one of the first) in your market. But... what if you are too late? What if one or more other people are positioned at the top already? What then? The answer is easy, just do the next best thing:

Be the First in a
"Sub Market"

In other words, if you sell healthy dog food, you can position yourself as the healthy dog food guy (or gal) JUST for Basenjis. Now, all the sudden, Basenji owners are not going to be satisfied with just any old healthy dog food. They ware going to want the one JUST for Basenjis.

And that's just one example.

The idea is to study—really study—your market and find an opening.

A way "in" nobody else is exploiting in your industry, area or niche.

It may take a lot of time and analysis, but it will be well worth it.

Crackerjack Selling Secret #99:
Take Off Your Mask

Imagine this for a second:

You are in the market for a new car. You pick the exact make and model you want and start looking around. You find two in your local paper—both the exact color, mileage, year, price, everything. They are like *identical twins*. So you meet with both of the owners and see about buying one of them. One of the car owners invites you over to see the car in their driveway. Nice people, kids playing outside, neighbors saying "hi!", you're offered a glass of lemonade, etc.

Then, you go to the other seller.

This guy makes you come to some abandoned shed in the middle of the night. When you get there, he is wearing sunglasses (at night). He tells you nothing about the background and history of the car. There is nobody else around to "vouch" for this guy (no smiling neighbors, family or friends).

Now, in this case, even though you are looking at two identical cars at identical prices, which person are you more likely to buy from?

My point?

As we saw with Crackerjack Selling Secret #1, all sales come down first and foremost to building *trust*. People buy from people they know, like and trust.

It really is as simple as that.

And if you want people to trust you—and therefore be more likely to BUY from you —

Take Off Your "Mask"

Be open and *transparent*.

For example, give your phone number, address, names of friends, etc. Let your customers know about your family, your dog and even some of your personal feelings and attitudes. Tell people the names of other people (especially if they are well known) who will *vouch* for you. Encourage them to talk with your OTHER customers. And anything else that will remove all the fear from whether or not you're some con man who will simply take their money and run.

Doing these small things make it very easy and "safe" to trust and do business with you.

Both of which help make selling a *breeze*.

Crackerjack Selling Secret #100:
The Yammer-Free Zone

Earlier, in <u>Crackerjack Selling Secrets #40</u> and <u>#93</u>, we talked about the importance of getting and keeping *attention*. How getting attention and then *keeping* it is mandatory for selling anything. Well, one way to do both (and this is getting increasingly important as our attention spans are reduced to gnat-like level by TV and the Internet), is to simply...

Get to the Point!

And *fast*.

Most people are extremely busy. They don't have time (or the attention span) for long "warm ups" or irrelevant tangents that have nothing to do with their most *urgent* problems and desires. They don't have the patience to listen to someone (or read a sales letter) that yammers on and on and on without getting to the point. And that "point" should, of course, be their problems and desires.

I know this seems almost too simple.

But it is extremely important. And if you want to keep someone's attention, and make it *easier* to buy from you than not buy from you…

Get to the Point!

Don't dilly-dally.

Don't dawdle.

And, whatever you do, don't waste your customers' time.

You would be surprised how much *just* doing this can increase your sales.

Crackerjack Selling Secret #101:
Burn the Training Wheels

And finally, we come "full circle" to the last, and final Crackerjack Selling secret:

Take off the
Training Wheels.

By that I mean, go out and USE what you've learned in this book. Practice them whenever you get a chance.

Use them with your customers, your prospects and even your friends and family (if for no other purpose than to practice "selling" them on going to a specific movie or restaurant they normally would not want to go to).

Seek out people you disagree with (*passionately*) on things, and try to "sell" them on your point of view.

Practice, practice, practice. It really DOES make perfect.

And the more you use these Crackerjack Selling Secrets, the more they become a *part* of you. Soon, they are like second nature and you do not have to even think about them (memory experts call this "unconscious competence"—like driving a car).

In fact, you will start to literally do them...

On Auto-Pilot!

As I said in the beginning, you do not have to memorize and use all 101 of these secrets. Just pick the ones that appeal to you, that you can apply to your business and method of selling (i.e. face to face, in print, etc.).

Always be honing and practicing what you learn in selling.

It's the "key" to success in anything in life—and especially in sales.

Acknowledgements

No book is written without help.

Not even a *short* one like this.

And I want to thank those who helped me with their insights, feedback and contributions. Some of the people below who "helped" me write this didn't even realize they were helping me (and some have no idea who I am, or are deceased).

But since I drew upon many of their teachings, wisdom and inspirations, I consider this as much their work as mine.

So, without further ado, I would like to thank Ken McCarthy, Gary Bencivenga, David Dutton, Gary Halbert, Eugene Schwartz, Jim Camp, Greg Perry, Doug D'Anna, Terry Dean, Rich Bryda, Daniel Levis, Nafis Noorali, Derek Scott, Tom "Big Al" Schreiter, Art Jonak, "Shameless" Shamus Brown, Fred Herman, Jim Yaghi, Robert Cialdini, Paul Hartunian, Gerry Spence, Mark Weiser, Joe Vitale, Mike Dillard, Ryan Healy, Bruce Barton, Dale Carnegie, Frank Bettger, John Anghelache, Dan Kennedy, Robert Collier, Matt Gillogly, Victor Cheng, Michael Senoff, Michel Fortin, Ray Edwards... and the *legions* of other expert selling and marketing geniuses whose teachings I have gleaned so much from over the years.

And finally, thank you, dear reader. For taking a chance on this book and on me. I sincerely hope you learned how to make more money and take more pleasure and joy from your work.

> ***For over 1000 pages of tips, dozens of hours of audio content and a free (digital) issue of the prestigious $97/month "Email Players" newsletter, go to:*

www.BenSettle.com

Disclosures and Disclaimers

All trademarks and service marks are the properties of their respective owners. All references to these properties are made solely for editorial purposes. Except for marks actually owned by the Author or the Publisher, no commercial claims are made to their use, and neither the Author nor the Publisher is affiliated with such marks in any way.

Unless otherwise expressly noted, none of the individuals or business entities mentioned herein has endorsed the contents of this book.

Limits of Liability & Disclaimers of Warranties

Because this book is a general educational information product, it is not a substitute for professional advice on the topics discussed in it.

The materials in this book are provided "as is" and without warranties of any kind either express or implied. The Author and the Publisher disclaim all warranties, express or implied, including, but not limited to, implied warranties of merchantability and fitness for a particular purpose. The Author and the Publisher do not warrant that defects will be corrected, or that any website or any server that makes this book available is free of viruses or other harmful components. The Author does not warrant or make any representations regarding the use or the results of the use of the materials in this book in terms of their correctness, accuracy, reliability, or otherwise. Applicable law may not allow the exclusion of implied warranties, so the above exclusion may not apply to you.

Under no circumstances, including, but not limited to, negligence, shall the Author or the Publisher be liable for any special or consequential damages that result from the use of, or the inability to use this book, even if the Author, the Publisher, or an authorized representative has been advised of the possibility of such damages. Applicable law may not allow the limitation or exclusion of liability or incidental or consequential damages, so the above limitation or exclusion may not apply to you. In no event shall the Author or Publisher total liability to you for all damages, losses, and causes of action (whether in contract, tort, including but not limited to, negligence or otherwise) exceed the amount paid by you, if any, for this book.

You agree to hold the Author and the Publisher of this book, principals, agents, affiliates, and employees harmless from any and all liability for all claims for damages due to injuries, including attorney fees and costs, incurred by you or caused to third parties by you, arising out of the products, services, and activities discussed in this book, excepting only claims for gross negligence or intentional tort.

You agree that any and all claims for gross negligence or intentional tort shall be settled solely by confidential binding arbitration per the American Arbitration Association's commercial arbitration rules. All arbitration must occur in the municipality where the Author's principal place of business is located. Arbitration fees and costs shall be split equally, and you are solely responsible for your own lawyer fees.

Facts and information are believed to be accurate at the time they were placed in this book. All data provided in this book is to be used for information purposes only. The information contained within is not intended to provide specific legal, financial, tax, physical or mental health advice, or any other advice whatsoever, for any individual or company and should not be relied upon in that regard. The services described are only offered in jurisdictions where they may be legally offered. Information provided is not all-inclusive, and is limited to information that is made available and such information should not be relied upon as all-inclusive or accurate.

For more information about this policy, please contact the Author at the e-mail address listed in the Copyright Notice at the front of this book.

IF YOU DO NOT AGREE WITH THESE TERMS AND EXPRESS CONDITIONS, DO NOT READ THIS BOOK. YOUR USE OF THIS BOOK, PRODUCTS, SERVICES, AND ANY PARTICIPATION IN ACTIVITIES MENTIONED IN THIS BOOK, MEAN THAT YOU ARE AGREEING TO BE LEGALLY BOUND BY THESE TERMS.

Affiliate Compensation & Material Connections Disclosure

This book may contain hyperlinks to websites and information created and maintained by other individuals and organizations. The Author and the Publisher do not control or guarantee the accuracy, completeness, relevance, or timeliness of any information or privacy policies posted on these linked websites.

You should assume that all references to products and services in this book are made because material connections exist between the Author or Publisher and the providers of the mentioned products and services ("Provider"). You should also assume that all hyperlinks within this book are affiliate links for (a) the Author, (b) the Publisher, or (c) someone else who is an affiliate for the mentioned products and services (individually and collectively, the "Affiliate").

The Affiliate recommends products and services in this book based in part on a good faith belief that the purchase of such products or services will help readers in general.

The Affiliate has this good faith belief because (a) the Affiliate has tried the product or service mentioned prior to recommending it or (b) the Affiliate has researched the reputation of the Provider and has made the decision to recommend the Provider's products or services based on the Provider's history of providing these or other products or services.

The representations made by the Affiliate about products and services reflect the Affiliate's honest opinion based upon the facts known to the Affiliate at the time this book was published.

Because there is a material connection between the Affiliate and Providers of products or services mentioned in this book, you should always assume that the Affiliate may be biased because of the Affiliate's relationship with a Provider and/or because the Affiliate has received or will receive something of value from a Provider.

Perform your own due diligence before purchasing a product or service mentioned in this book.

The type of compensation received by the Affiliate may vary. In some instances, the Affiliate may receive complimentary products (such as a review copy), services, or money from a Provider prior to mentioning the Provider's products or services in this book.

In addition, the Affiliate may receive a monetary commission or non-monetary compensation when you take action by clicking on a hyperlink in this book. This includes, but is not limited to, when you purchase a product or service from a Provider after clicking on an affiliate link in this book.

Earnings & Income Disclaimers - No Earnings Projections, Promises or Representations

For purposes of these disclaimers, the term "Author" refers individually and collectively to the author of this book and to the affiliate (if any) whose affiliate links are embedded in this book.

You recognize and agree that the Author and the Publisher have made no implications, warranties, promises, suggestions, projections, representations or guarantees whatsoever to you about future prospects or earnings, or that you will earn any money, with respect to your purchase of this book, and that the Author and the Publisher have not authorized any such projection, promise, or representation by others.

Any earnings or income statements, or any earnings or income examples, are only estimates of what you *might* earn. There is no assurance you will do as well as stated in any examples. If you rely upon any figures provided, you must accept the entire risk of not doing as well as the information provided. This applies whether the earnings or income examples are monetary in nature or pertain to advertising credits which may be earned (whether such credits are convertible to cash or not).

There is no assurance that any prior successes or past results as to earnings or income (whether monetary or advertising credits, whether convertible to cash or not) will apply, nor can any prior successes be used, as an indication of your future success or results from any of the information, content, or strategies. Any and all claims or representations as to income or earnings (whether monetary or advertising credits, whether convertible to cash or not) are not to be considered as "average earnings".

Testimonials & Examples

Testimonials and examples in this book are exceptional results, do not reflect the typical purchaser's experience, do not apply to the average person and are not intended to represent or guarantee that anyone will achieve the same or similar results. Where specific income or earnings (whether monetary or advertising credits, whether convertible to cash or not), figures are used and attributed to a specific individual or business, that individual or business has earned that amount. There is no assurance that you will do as well using the same information or strategies. If you rely on the specific income or earnings figures used, you must accept all the risk of not doing as well. The described experiences are atypical. Your financial results are likely to differ from those described in the testimonials.

The Economy

The economy, where you do business, on a national and even worldwide scale, creates additional uncertainty and economic risk. An economic recession or depression might negatively affect your results.

Your Success or Lack of It

Your success in using the information or strategies provided in this book depends on a variety of factors. The Author and the Publisher have no way of knowing how well you will do because they do not know you, your background, your work ethic, your dedication, your motivation, your desire, or your business skills or practices. Therefore, neither the Author nor the Publisher guarantees or implies that you will get rich, that you will do as well, or that you will have any earnings (whether monetary or advertising credits, whether convertible to cash or not), at all.

Businesses and earnings derived therefrom involve unknown risks and are not suitable for everyone. You may not rely on any information presented in this book or otherwise provided by the Author or the Publisher, unless you do so with the knowledge and understanding that you can experience significant losses (including, but not limited to, the loss of any monies paid to purchase this book and/or any monies spent setting up, operating, and/or marketing your business activities, and further, that you may have no earnings at all (whether monetary or advertising credits, whether convertible to cash or not).

Forward-Looking Statements

Materials in this book may contain information that includes or is based upon forward-looking statements within the meaning of the securities litigation reform act of 1995. Forward-looking statements give the Author's expectations or forecasts of future events. You can identify these statements by the fact that they do not relate strictly to historical or current facts. They use words such as "anticipate," "estimate," "expect," "project," "intend," "plan," "believe," and other words and terms of similar meaning in connection with a description of potential earnings or financial performance.

Any and all forward looking statements here or on any materials in this book are intended to express an opinion of earnings potential. Many factors will be important in determining your actual results and no guarantees are made that you will achieve results similar to the Author or anybody else. In fact, no guarantees are made that you will achieve any results from applying the Author's ideas, strategies, and tactics found in this book.

Purchase Price

Although the Publisher believes the price is fair for the value that you receive, you understand and agree that the purchase price for this book has been arbitrarily set by the Publisher. This price bears no relationship to objective standards.

Due Diligence

You are advised to do your own due diligence when it comes to making any decisions. Use caution and seek the advice of qualified professionals before acting upon the contents of this book or any other information. You shall not consider any examples, documents, or other content in this book or otherwise provided by the Author or Publisher to be the equivalent of professional advice.

The Author and the Publisher assume no responsibility for any losses or damages resulting from your use of any link, information, or opportunity contained in this book or within any other information disclosed by the Author or the Publisher in any form whatsoever.

YOU SHOULD ALWAYS CONDUCT YOUR OWN INVESTIGATION (PERFORM DUE DILIGENCE) BEFORE BUYING PRODUCTS OR SERVICES FROM ANYONE OFFLINE OR VIA THE INTERNET. THIS INCLUDES PRODUCTS AND SERVICES SOLD VIA HYPERLINKS EMBEDDED IN THIS BOOK.

Made in United States
North Haven, CT
15 March 2024

50026667R00093